GRIDLOCK

By Payne Edwards

Why We're In It
AND
How To Get Out

SIGNALMAN PUBLISHING

Gridlock
Why We're In It and How to Get Out
by Payne Edwards

Signalman Publishing   2012
www.signalmanpublishing.com
email: info@signalmanpublishing.com
Kissimmee, Florida

Cover photo, design and interior design by Joel Ramnaraine.

ISBN: 978-1-935991-49-6

Library of Congress Control Number: 2012933094

Signalman
Publishing

Printed in the United States of America

*In memory of and dedicated to
my father and all others who support
and defend the Constitution.*

TABLE OF CONTENTS

PREFACE

Occupy Wall Street, the TEA Party, the outpouring of support for hope and change. Contrasted with the voters' discontent with American governance, national politicians are stuck in a bipolar partisan deadlock while the country continues to plunge toward insolvency and nothing sane is done. The conventional wisdom is that this is because there is an ideological divide that must first be decided before the government has a plurality to take it in one direction or the other.

Voters don't look at government like federal-level partisans do. The national parties and the national media think of the federal government when they say government. To the national crowd, state government is an unknown minor league, and local government is a simpleton enterprise that takes out the trash, promotes suburban sprawl or urban wasteland, and enacts goofy ordnances. On the other hand, voters look up and see government in three layers, local, then state, then federal. City, town and county residents see their tax dollars going to all three layers. They see lots of real estate tax dollars going to local education, local services and facilities, and lots of state tax dollars going to higher education, human and health services, and state-wide facilities. They wince but accept it when their localities take on debt for needed capital improvements, like new school buildings, new fire trucks and improved local roads, knowing their taxes will probably go up. Teachers see cutbacks in payrolls and students see reductions in services and subsidies, and complain. But state and local officials calmly explain the reality of balancing expenditures against revenues. At the local and state level, the competition between public need and the public fisc is handled politically in an understandable and open way, based on fiscal reality, although sometimes with heated dialogue.

Then the feds ride into town, flush with cash. It is cash from other people; to state and local folks, it is free money. It seems to come from an inexhaustible source. Federal officials proclaim compassion, they offer help, they argue that a country as rich as ours needs to leverage its wealth for the common good. It has worked this way for decades, and never seemed the worse for wear.

Except, recently, some of the locals grew suspicious of the federal money train. And others grew aware that, somehow, a few were making out like bandits at the expense of all the others. And then both groups realized that the federal government was shipping out small cash amounts to pay off some individuals and groups for votes while shoveling the big bucks to the connected. Both groups have realized that American governance, with the preeminence of the federal government, was both going broke while enriching a few, and only paying lip service to the people.

Our current situation is not an ideological divide about the proper limits of government. It is a divide between reality and propaganda[1], either far-left or far-right, with the typical American caught in between. It is a divide between those who believe, or have been led to believe, that there is a never ending supply of free money, and increasing numbers of people across the country who believe that the current level of national debt is dangerous, and increasing the level of debt threatens the future. It is a divide between people able to exploit the federal government, and the vast majority who suffer under its weight. It is a divide between those bought off by federal cash, and those who are paying the bill.

Americans of all stripes believe in the need for good, proactive and sometimes protective government. They don't believe in limiting government to some bare libertarian minimum. They believe in governance that is properly sized and judiciously empowered. They also don't believe in expanding government to manage the economy and to direct social activity. They believe in governance that is lean but sufficiently protective of its citizens' interests.

While local and state governments are generally meeting Americans' expectations, the federal government is failing. It has become a bloated money pit, administered by two angry political machines interested only in winning a governing majority. The federal government is failing miserably to do its part.

But it is not the federal government alone that needs treatment. The system of American governance as a whole is suffering. Fortunately, it is not a terminal illness. Surgical instruments embedded in the Constitution are ready to be used by motivated, popularly supported practitioners. The many hands of nursemaids found in state governments are ready to get to work when a sufficiently broad popular base comes together to empower them. The American system of governance is ready to be revived by restoring balance to the local, state and federal elements which must work together harmoniously for the country to flourish and for its people to prosper.

This essay offers a vision for restoring balance to the American system of governance. It presents specific recommendations for implementing change. Being the work of one person, it undoubtedly needs to be thoroughly analyzed and vetted by others. But, the author's motivation is not to promote any particular political ideology, nor to promote either main political party. Rather, it is a framework to make American governance again work for the general welfare, while still allowing, and even encouraging, advocates and ideologues of all persuasions to participate in the political process. Is it designed to loosen the grip of the national parties on the federal government? Absolutely it is. But is it designed to empower or legitimize either party over the other? No it is not; in fact it is hoped that it de-powers both national level Republicans and Democrats equally. Its primary motivation is to restore the American system of governance to one whose main focus is to be representative of all the people and one working for their general betterment.

*   *   *

This book was written to answer two questions. Why did we reach gridlock, and how do we get out of it? The book analyzes the 'why' from a detached perspective, with the premise that most political leaders of all political persuasions have sought to do what is best for the country. It suggests a 'how' that addresses the root causes that have created today's gridlock.

INTRODUCTION

Government is competent when all who compose it work as trustees for the whole people. It can make constant progress when it keeps abreast of all the facts. It can obtain justified support and legitimate criticism when the people receive true information of all that government does.
—President Franklin Roosevelt, 1937 Inaugural Address

American society, culture and the economy are in the 21st century while American governance is instituted in 20th century constructs and practices. Such governance cannot be competent nor can it make progress, particularly when it lacks public confidence. At the federal level, in its critical responsibilities of borrowing money, regulating the value of money, and regulating commerce, it has brought the country to potential economic crisis. In the broader scheme, American governance has failed the general welfare of the people while giving advantage to large corporations and narrow special interests, and is an incompetent agent for promoting its citizen's well-being in an increasingly competitive and complex world.

American governance has grown distant from the American people. America's public resources have been misspent and misused, misdirected to the benefit of the powerful and the favored while underfunding broad-based enterprises that benefit the general public. America's economic potential and its future wealth have been put at great risk by persistent federal deficit spending and the accumulation of an unsustainable level of debt.

Millions of Americans, regrettably, agree that this is the current sad state of America's affairs. American's are increasingly concerned that their innate optimism is being shaved away as each passing year brings not improving prospects, but rather declining national health and vitality. Rather than providing leadership and taking action to promote the general welfare, Americans see political leaders mired in governmental gridlock, and politicians deadlocked by partisanship and addicted to campaigning.

Historically, this is not new. The late 1800s and early 1900s were a time of great national societal and economic change which American governance was increasingly incapable of handling. But from the 1880's and into the very early 1900s, when elected officials were politically incapable of making needed reforms to governance, there arose a popular consensus for structural governmental change which ultimately compelled political action. During the popular movements of the early 1900s, the people started clamoring for more active American governance. Back then, like today, most political party leaders offered only minor adjustments to the status quo. But, unlike today, back then a few men and women of national standing were able to integrate growing popular notions for change and condense them into an articulately stated vision of what American government needed to become, and how it not only would address the failings of the day, but also how it would preserve American political ideals and foundations of the past.

This essay offers a vision for today that might again rally broad popular support. It envisions a new system of American governance that forces political leadership to deal effectively with today's challenges, that compels leaders to balance Americans' personal freedom with the power of government, that empowers leaders to advance society and support communities without simply redistributing wealth, and that encourages fiscal discipline. It is a vision for the majority of voters, whether Democratic, Republican or Independent.

It is not a vision for restructuring, reforming or remaking the federal government; it is a vision for restoring representative American governance.

The primary failing of American governance that provoked the Progressive era in the early 1900s was the failure of state governments. In the late 19th century, state governments held the preponderance of governing power in the United States. In a time of great social and economic change, state governments failed to react. The Progressive Era vision was to expand the power and reach of the federal government to address problems that had become fundamentally national level problems, generated by the shift from local economies to a system of integrated national commerce and finance, accompanied with the rise of concentrated wealth in industrialists.

The primary failing of American governance today is the federal government. The federal government has reached a level of over-expansion that has resulted in a governmental system that is incapable of effective governance. Over-expansion of the federal government has been an evolutionary political development. The federal government today is set on the foundation of the Progressive Era's federal structure, one molded for the industrial age. Societal and economic changes that occurred throughout the 20th century caused further expansion. Federal government grew by modifying or adding programs and policies to a federal government whose basic structure was becoming increasingly outdated with respect to economic and societal reality. In other words, the federal government grew while continuingly adding to a basis that was becoming more irrelevant. The growth was like trying to continually modify a 1909 Model T Ford year after year and turn it into a 1999 Ford Explorer. Expansion over the last hundred years was not spurred on by either political party or by any presidential administration simply for the sake of concentrating power, as some would believe. It was instead the natural result of a political system that loosened most of the restraints that could limit the accumulation of power in the federal government.

The over-expansion of the federal government has had deleterious consequences. One direct consequence is that the federal government has lost focus on its core responsibilities because it has diverted its attention towards many more things. Other consequences include governance that is both ponderous and cumbersome, undisciplined fiscal policy and practice, and a system that empowers corporations and special interests at the expense of promoting the general welfare. Over-expansion simply spurs the federal government to expand even further, and with the centralization of power, Congressmen and the President are more and more open to corruption. Finally, an over-expansive federal government hamstrings state and local governments in making decisions, in being responsive, and being able to be innovative.

A package of reforms includes Constitutional Amendments, state Constitution Amendments and federal and state legislation. I believe that the implementation of all these reforms would provide the greatest benefit. Adoption of any of them, however, would be an improvement. The lessons of the Progressive Era are instructive again. Driven by what became overwhelming popular support, a host of Constitutional Amendments, new laws and new executive orders were implemented in the short span of a few years that set American governance on a new course.

The specific reforms are explained in detail later. But the primary objective is to rebalance governing between the federal and state governments, to empower state governments to provide innovative, effective, and proactive representative government, and to refocus the federal government on its core Constitutional responsibilities in a fiscally sound construct.

This next point is very important. It is vital to address a concern that has reached mythical status before continuing. It is the myth that "states' rights" means oppressive, regressive or inattentive government; that only the federal government can protect all citizens and promote progress. This view is a canard promoted by those seeking to concentrate political power, not to promote effective popular government. First, to think that the people who become federal officials are somehow more capable or inclined to promote positive government than people who become state officials is simply illogical. Second, this myth assumes that federal governmental processes, knowledge and understanding of societal dynamics, and ability to both enact and implement policy is superior to state governments. There is no basis for this assertion. Finally, federal action to restore the civil rights of black Americans in the 20th century is frequently cited as a justification for federal government activism. Through state and local laws, states had disenfranchised black voters and legalized segregation. These state practices violated specific individual rights that were enumerated in the Constitution's fourteenth Amendment, which further explicitly prohibited the states from enacting discriminating laws. The President and the Congress had to take direct action against and within the states to defend the Constitution, as they were empowered to do by the Constitution itself. When the states chose to violate the Constitution, the federal government had to end the illegal state measures. This was in fact a finite and proper exercise of federal government power. It is not a precedent for the federal government to intervene whenever the Congress or the President choose in order to change state laws they don't like, or to replace state laws with federal laws solely to enhance their power.

The guiding vision of these reforms is to get societal and community government closer to the people by restoring to state and local governments the power and authority that the federal government has absorbed over the last century, to impose meaningful fiscal restraints on all levels of government, and to curtail the power of corporations and special interests over political processes.

Here, I ask the reader to pause, and give thoughtful consideration to this vision and the intent of the reforms necessary for the vision. I particularly ask that die-hard Republicans and Democrats grant a hearing. This is not a call for terminating or curtailing laws, policies and programs that have made progress in promoting society and communities, and which most Americans support.[2] It is intended to shift much societal and community governance from the federal government to state governments. Republican partisans will object, citing the need for "limited government." Democratic partisans will object, citing the need for "active government." In truth, the vision supports both limited government and active government. It envisions a prudently limited federal government, and active, but fiscally-sound state governments. If you are convinced that only the (debt-ridden, gridlocked, Wall-Street-loving, bloated, IRS-sporting) federal government can handle today's problems and governance in general, stop reading. If you are convinced that only by severely limiting the power of both the federal and state governments (and ending all regulations, safety-nets, progressive taxation, public education, environmental standards), stop reading. For the rest of us, the vision hinges on this: are state governments willing and able to assume a significantly expanded role. I obviously believe that they can. I also think most Governors and state legislators feel the same. And, there is also one group that believed passionately that the states are more than capable: our Founding Fathers. They believed that states would promote progress for their people, while a federal government of limited societal and communitarian power would promote national progress in which the states could prosper.

Specific reforms include several Amendments to the Constitution. One Amendment should clarify the Commerce Clause and limit the federal government's ability to regulate all economic activity. Another Amendment should restate the Tenth Amendment whereby the powers delegated to the federal government are given clear limits and boundaries. Third, the Constitution should include a finance Amendment, fashioned after that found in many state constitutions. It should mandate a balanced annual operating budget where annual expenditures are limited to anticipated annual revenues, a separate Capital Account budget including limits on total capital investment levels and debt, and the outlines of the annual processes for formulating and then executing the budget. This would not be a balanced budget Amendment that simply limits federal spending to some monetary level. Fourth, choosing U.S. Senators should be returned to state legislatures in order to return the Senate's motivation to serve the interests of state governments. Fifth, an Amendment is needed to strip from Congress some of the powers it has insidiously assumed, and whose primary purpose was to give Representatives, Senators and the President more control. The Amendment would prohibit federal involvement with education, prohibit federal tax credits, and end "revenue sharing." All told, these Amendments would rebalance the American system of governance.

Other reforms do not necessarily require the strength of a Constitutional Amendment. Today's obscene federal tax code is already garnering nationwide support for major reform. Congress should revamp the federal tax code (with the expectation that states would follow suit). States should adopt a two-part Amendment to their state Constitutions. To reduce cost, improve efficiency and enhance innovation, states should adopt the positive example of Nebraska by shrinking their legislature to a single body with fewer representatives, and mandate non-partisan elections and non-partisan control of the legislative body.

These reforms don't give an edge to either major political party. Nor do they promote one special interest group over another. The reforms do favor traditional American political ideologies and philosophies, both left and right. These reforms would leave plenty of room for Americanized socialists, liberals, conservatives and libertarians to try to advance their ideas and agendas in the political arena.

Interest groups and individuals who seek to impose, nation-wide, a particular belief or to implement a specific agenda will fight these reforms. So will political party members who seek to enact "comprehensive plans" for national-level initiatives since they will find it more difficult to advance their designs. In fact, almost every national organization will mobilize to counter these reforms because the reforms would diminish their power. Probably the only support for these reforms will come from beyond the Beltway, from the general public and their state and local elected representatives.

These reforms would most likely make individual states, in some ways, significantly different from one another. Each state would have more authority and resources to evolve politically in a way that leverages its strengths and promotes its unique cultural and societal character. But all the states would remain united under a still-strong federal government. Enhancing state control at the expense of federal power would be a cause for regret by some and a reason for delight by others. But our country has never been, simply, America. It is the United States of America.

THE PRESENT CONDITION OF AMERICAN GOVERNANCE

Most Americans believe in government. They expect government to provide effective community services, to encourage economic growth and to promote the general welfare, while at the same time expecting it to safeguard individual liberty, freedom and equal opportunity. Americans support proactive and powerful government, at the national, state or local level, where it is necessary and appropriate to secure national, state or community interests that are popularly supported. They support and expect national, state or community government to assume broad power to respond to national, state or local emergencies, but to shed power and control when the emergency is resolved.

The American system of government is distributed among representative federal, state and local governments, each having specific assigned responsibilities and powers which are prescribed in written constitutions or charters. Most Americans believe that this network of governments has served the country and communities well since American independence.

Starting with the Bill of Rights, Americans have supported modifying the federal government in order to better promote the general welfare. It has been more than a century since Theodore Roosevelt called for a New Nationalism during the 1912 presidential campaign. Roosevelt's arguments for greater federal action would sound eerily familiar to many today. They included excessive and corrupting influence in politics by corporations and Wall Street, the need to regulate the financial system to improve stability, measures to keep special interests subordinate to the general welfare, and progressive income taxes and estate taxes to rectify the accumulation of great wealth by the few. The early twentieth century Progressive movement produced federal financial regulatory agencies, launched the conservation movement, and spawned the federal income tax[3].

Federal expansion continued throughout the twentieth century with the addition of Social Security in the 1930s, Medicare and Medicaid in the 1960s, and the addition of new Cabinet departments and agencies in the 1960s and the 1970s.

Today, there is growing restlessness that the federal government is in crisis. The restless are concerned that the federal government is addicted to deficits, that it is imposing regulations which inhibit equal opportunity and economic growth, and that it is ineffective at controlling financial markets. The restless are found in both political parties.

When we think of governance, we need to make a distinction between the outcomes we want from our governmental system and the outputs we expect of the federal, state and local governments themselves. Except for a few subjects of bipolar disagreement, such as abortion, the national (Presidential) platforms of the two political parties are remarkably similar in terms of what Americans need and expect. Both want a strong national defense and support for veterans, energy independence, health care reform, environmental protection, reforming government to serve the people, etc. In other words, both Democrats and Republicans want similar positive developments in the nation's general welfare and prosperity. And national-level politicians of both parties generally ascribe to the need for the federal government to play an active role in advancing positive developments, whether the federal government is the agent that promotes outcomes (generally Republicans), or is the agent that achieves desired effects through specific governmental outputs (generally Democrats).

The power of the federal government to do things, whether in encouraging outcomes or in enacting specific legislative outputs, is derived from the Constitution. All Americans look to the Constitution as the definitive arbiter of the authority of the federal government.

The preamble of the Constitution tersely prescribes the functions and the authority of the federal government: "…to provide for the common defence, promote the general Welfare, and secure the Blessings of Liberty to ourselves and our Posterity." The Con-

stitution gives the Congress specific responsibilities, the enumerated powers, in Article I, Section 8. The most important of these in
terms of their effect on citizens include coining money, regulating
commerce among the states, establishing the post office, organizing
the armed forces and maintaining a navy, and to govern the District
of Columbia and federal property. The Tenth Amendment limits the
federal government's power to only what is in the Constitution, and
requires that all other governmental power be held by the states or
by individual citizens.

Despite the Constitution's limits, the federal government has
significantly expanded its power and its activities in the last one hundred years. Little of this expansion was accomplished by amending
the Constitution. Steadily and ponderously, the federal government
has become involved in areas seemingly far outside the enumerated powers assigned to the federal government by the Constitution.
Some of this expansion was supported by court decisions, but much
of it was done simply by expansive legislation or by executive order.
The federal government's growth has become generally accepted
and actively supported by both national political parties.

Congress passed many laws in the twentieth century which resulted in great numbers of ambitious regulations. Most of the laws
and regulations have an economic aspect. Many regulate industrial, commercial, agricultural and financial activity. Others regulate
general economic activity of organizations or individuals. Others
regulate the flow of goods and services. In a steady succession of
opinions, the Supreme Court has granted Congress nearly unlimited
power to regulate all aspects of economic activity.

The Courts cite Article I, Section 8 of the Constitution as the basis for giving Congress free rein to regulate and control economic
activity. Known as the "Commerce Clause," a portion of Article I,
Section 8 reads, "The Congress shall have the power to regulate
Commerce with foreign Nations, and among the several states, and
with the Indian tribes."

In Federalist Paper Number 45, James Madison reflected the understanding of early Americans who drafted and ratified the Constitution.

The powers delegated by the proposed Constitution to the Federal government are few and defined. Those which are to remain in the State governments are numerous and indefinite. The former will be exercised principally on external objects, as war, peace, negotiation, and foreign commerce; with which last the power of taxation will, for the most part, be connected. The powers reserved to the several States will extend to all the objects which, in the ordinary course of affairs, concern the lives, liberties, and properties of the people, and the internal order, improvement and prosperity of the State.

If the new Constitution be examined with accuracy and candor, it will be found that the change which it proposes consists much less in the addition of NEW POWERS to the Union than in the invigoration of its ORIGINAL POWERS. The regulation of commerce, it is true, is a new power; but that seems to be an addition few oppose *and from which no apprehensions are entertained.* [Italics added]

What the Constitution identifies as commerce, today we would call the economy. And the economy is in all things and everywhere. To use Hamilton's term in Federalist Number 11, the "veins of commerce" stretch through and across the states in ever growing ways. The Supreme Court has consistently decided that defining what commerce is and how it is best regulated are beyond the ability of courts to determine. Commerce and the economy comprise numerous complex issues, and appropriate regulation is fundamentally a political issue. The Supreme Court has further found that Congress's power in regulating commerce is, as Chief Justice Stone opined in 1942, "plenary and complete in itself, may be exercised to its utmost extent, and acknowledges no limitations other than are prescribed in the Constitution."[4] Because there are no prescriptions active in the Constitution that limit or define Congress' power to regulate commerce, Congressional authority with respect to regulating any aspect of commerce, or anything related to commerce, is essentially unbridled.

The debate on the Constitutionality of continuing federal government activism and expansion will continue as the courts adjudicate new federal legislation, the recent Patient Protection and Affordable Care Act (PPACA) being the most recent issue. But the courts will wrestle with difficulty to reach a Constitutional basis for limiting the federal government's legislative authority for regulating the economy. Even though in 1995 the Supreme Court set some limits on what can be regulated under the rubric of contributing to "commerce," the Supreme Court's opinion was based on what constitutes the legal extent of commerce, not that Congress's authority to regulate commerce is, in any way, constrained by the Constitution.[5]

The Tenth Amendment states that the powers not delegated to the federal government are reserved to the states, or to the people. But the Tenth Amendment doesn't reference commerce explicitly. So, defining commerce, and hence what the federal government can regulate, remains an open question, and thus requires a political decision. And the Supreme Court has said that Congress has unlimited power to determine how the word commerce is defined.

Unless a new Amendment is added to the Constitution which better defines commerce or limits Congress's power to regulate the economy, it is only the Congress itself that has the power to reduce or reverse the expansion of the federal government. Even if the Supreme Court breaks from prior precedent and finds that there are limits to Congress's power to regulate aspects of commerce, or the economy, the issue can only be marginally confined or restrained, because the Constitution's grant of power to Congress to regulate the economy is broad, and the reach of the economy itself is exceedingly difficult to define in legal terms.

After nearly two and a half centuries, the U.S. federal government has evolved to become the dominant player in the American system, controlled by the national Democratic and Republican parties. The national Democratic Party leadership is committed to the status quo and seeks to further expand the reach of the federal government. Except for the Reagan presidency and the Republican Congress in the middle 1990s, the national Republican Party has also supported expansion of the federal government. But the 2010 election witnessed a popular uprising of voters who were suddenly aroused by a rapidly growing debt, and who saw the federal government not only doing nothing to reduce spending, but also enacting laws that accelerated spending, while passing laws and regulations that seemed to stifle rather than encourage economic growth.

The popular uprising has been labeled the TEA Party, adopting an acronym for, "taxed enough already." Some voters have accepted the label and organized groups to become a true grassroots effort that influences politics.

Those who associate with the TEA party believe that the solution to reducing the federal debt, and deficit spending, requires a hard line against any tax increases, in any form. They believe that only with a hard line against tax increases will Congress be forced to control spending. Outside the TEA Party there are many voters who agree that federal spending is out of control, but they are not adamantly opposed to increasing taxes. If it were a grass roots party, it could adopt the acronym of SEA Party – Spent Enough Already. Many Americans, previously oblivious, have suddenly started paying attention to the federal debt and its causes. They have realized the simple fact that federal spending which relies on borrowing 40% each year is unsustainable; that over-spending is the problem. The SEA Party sympathizer isn't averse to raising taxes to pay down the debt—but only with a solid assurance that additional taxes won't simply go to more spending. TEA Party members are convinced that the Congressional addiction to spending can only be restrained by freezing the level of revenues, and relying on the fact that a growing national debt will ultimately hit a fiscal ceiling that makes it impossible to incur more debt. But SEA Party thinkers are uncomfortable with this approach because they fear the impact on the economy and financial markets on reaching a too-high debt level. They believe that, with real pressure, Congress can rein in spending, and maybe even with judicious tax increases, can take control of the national debt.

The TEA Party influence has been absorbed by the Republican

Party. Some Republicans in Congress are actively supporting efforts to limit spending by the federal government. But support for reducing spending does not mean that all Republicans are committed to curtailing the reach of the federal government, which has made TEA party support for the Republican Party tenuous.

In the summer of 2011, the Occupy movement erupted. Although harder to nail down in terms of a political or policy theme, the Occupy movement reflected the angst of many about the direction the country was taking its people. But the Occupy movement has been united by one theme: the bankers and financial corporations were making lots of money while the vast majority of Americans were not, and that the federal government was responsible for the mess.

Neither national political party has absorbed the Occupy movement. A few Democratic politicians have connected with it, from a distance. It remains an orphan of the body politic. But that doesn't diminish its momentum to generate popular sentiment looking for substantive reform.

For decades, state and local officials have bemoaned the onslaught of federal mandates and regulations. Most states accept federal dollars reluctantly. The additional revenue comes with unpopular or inappropriate strings attached. Often, federal dollars mandate state or local matching funds, forcing state or local governments to increase taxes or to divert funds from other areas. In some instances, when a state rejects federal funds because it opposes the associated federal rules or regulations that come with them, more funding is diverted to other states, leaving the taxpayers of the state bewildered that more off their tax dollars are going to support something that they don't want. State governments are increasingly fighting against federal government intrusion into what state officials see as areas that are their prerogative. State and local officials are joining average voters and popular movements in demanding change to restrain an increasingly all-powerful federal government.

The TEA Party and the Occupy movement are illustrative of general and growing concern with what the federal government has become. Many other Americans are becoming more informed and increasingly more suspicious of federal officials, and more worried about the federal debt and deficits. Almost no one on the left, on the right or in between believes that the federal government can fix itself in today's political context. Some blame the two-party system, or the federal system of governance, or the Constitutional construct of the federal government. Others posit that the Constitution is fundamentally sound, but its strictures have been ignored or perversely exploited. No matter the explanation for the federal government's malaise, no one can suggest a viable political solution. Theories, rationalizations and partisan accusations abound; compelling ideas for a way out of the morass are few, and are either trite or tyrannical.

National political leaders aren't providing a substantive vision for restoring American governance and American vitality. President Obama rode the wave of public discomfort with refreshing promises of real change in governance. Two years later, astonishing mid-term national elections expressed continued discontentment.

There seems to be no way out of a left-right, up-down, yin-yang dichotomy that can never deliver real reform. There seems no way to square the circle of reversing overspending and reducing the debt while at the same time not harming the economy and maintaining popular government programs and policies.

There seems to be no way because everyone is looking to political leaders to "fix" the federal government. But the federal government has evolved to the point that effective American governance cannot be restored by rearranging the deck chairs of the federal government, or by centralizing more or different powers in the federal government. During the earlier Progressive Era, the people insisted on a new vision of governance, and the people eventually forced the political system to adopt major reforms. Fortunately, despite the great power wielded by national party leaders through a growing federal government, the people still have the political strength and Constitutional means for changing their system of governance.

CONSEQUENCES OF EXPANSIVE FEDERAL GOVERNANCE

Before considering the package of reforms which are needed to restore health to the American system of governance, it is important to examine the consequences that have accrued from an over-expansive federal government.

The century-long expansion of the federal Government has resulted in substantive developments which have fundamentally changed the American system of governance. I identify those which I believe have had the greatest impact, and describe their consequences. In the aggregate, all of the developments have had one overarching result. The American system of governance has become less and less representative of the people, less and less focused on promoting the general welfare, and generally unconcerned with preserving individual freedom and liberty.

The primary effect of an expansive federal government is that it defocuses the Congress and the President from effectively managing the federal government's core duties and responsibilities prescribed by the Constitution. This alone is a significant consequence. But shifting its focus toward a host of other matters has generated secondary effects that have had adverse consequences in other ways. Excess expansion of the federal Government:

- Promotes the interests of corporations and special interests.
- Hinders proactive and responsive governance.
- Encourages deficit spending and high levels of public debt.
- Propels greater expansion of the federal government.

A tertiary effect has been to reduce the capacity of state governments to promote progress and to govern effectively by mandating rules, by limiting state governmental authority, and by reducing the available state and local revenue base. The net of these effects is a distorted system of federal governance that is growing ever more tilted in favor of corporations and special interests and ambivalent to the welfare of the general population. Finally, the product of these effects is the polarization of the two national political parties.

Primary Effect

The federal government has been doing a poor job at what the Constitution says it should do. Failure to control immigration and naturalization has resulted in millions of undocumented non-citizens. The air traffic control system is obsolete. The interstate highway system is inadequately maintained and lacks sufficient capacity. International trade is plagued with inefficiencies; the regulations for interstate commerce are burdensome and overly complex. The laws for exercising federal power are ponderous and voluminous, requiring a proliferation of attorneys to interpret and comply with them. The tax code is obscene. The military seems to work, but its cost is exorbitant and its bureaucracy is a mess. The Constitution gives Congress alone the power to establish post offices, and the postal service is going broke. The patent system is plagued with delays and patent laws are not keeping pace with the advancement of technology and discovery[6]. Among its enumerated powers, Congress seems efficient at only the first: "To borrow Money on the credit of the United States."[7]

It would bloat this essay to fully describe all the problems and inefficiencies of the federal government in doing what the Constitution says it should do. Volumes have been written which document the sad state of affairs in this area, including a never-ending stream of Congressional studies which highlight poor programs and slipshod implementation of federal policies. However, there are two relatively recent examples that highlight Congress's poor record of carrying out the responsibilities assigned to it by the Constitution. Both concern regulation of the economy.

Congress's foray into the national housing market, even though the Courts have said that the commerce clause gives Congress the authority, has been a disaster. This is particularly illustrative both of

Congress's inability to do its job, and of what happens when Congress is given license to exercise powers that were never intended to be granted by the Commerce Clause. In their Resolutions ratifying the original Constitution, four states recommended immediately adding an Amendment worded as follows: "That Congress shall erect no Company of Merchants with exclusive advantages of Commerce." This Amendment was not adopted. In deciding whether to add this Amendment to the proposed Bill of Rights, the first Congress probably thought the Constitution already prohibited Congress from erecting a company. In hindsight, it is probably too bad this Amendment wasn't adopted. It would have stopped Congress from chartering Fannie Mae and Freddie Mac and putting these companies squarely in the center of the nation's mortgage business. Whatever the intentions of Congress in improving the housing market for all Americans, most agree that this Congressional effort was very harmful to the economy and resulted in directly harming many individual Americans.

Congress's regulation of financial markets has been inadequate and overly cumbersome for decades. The national financial markets are commercial activities that most would agree are subject to Congressional regulation. The problem is that Congress has generally established a system of regulation that relies on the threat of penalties to correct or deter wrongdoing, rather than establishing regulated frameworks that encourage healthy financial institutions and sound financial activities while also providing for accountability when the system is abused. Much of Congress's focus has been on political grandstanding, using emotionally charged hearings or scolding speeches, rather than doing the much harder work of becoming expert on the system it is charged to regulate and then establishing appropriate effective regulation that promotes the national economy and protects the general population.

Suffice to say that it is a full time job for Congress and the President to refocus the federal government on its core Constitutional responsibilities. But Representatives, Senators and the President don't have the time to attend to their core responsibilities because they are too distracted by attending to other things. Nor are there political incentives for them to stay focused on the core responsibilities. With the federal Government now engaged in almost every aspect of local and state-level activities, elected federal officials attract as many votes based on extracurricular endeavors as on Constitutionally-mandated responsibilities.

Secondary Effects
Corporations and Special Interests

The Progressive Era of the early 20th century had as its primary motivation to rein in the robber barons of the time. A relative handful of industrialists had monopolized entire industries and amassed huge corporations to exploit the monopolies. Ever since then, the stereotypical view of corporations is one of huge, greedy, privately-owned special interests which are all-powerful, and must be tightly regulated to prevent them from corrupting government.

American corporations today are not comparable to the megacorporations of the late 1800s. Nonetheless, most Americans still view large corporations with suspicion; some view them with open contempt. Corporations employ lots of lobbyists and lawyers to engage Congressional staff and administration officials. Many make significant campaign contributions to individuals and to political parties. Corporations devote significant resources to influence the federal government, whether to ensure that laws and regulations favor their particular business interests, to solicit favorable tax breaks or to win federal contracts. Being in the business of business, what we today refer to as private sector corporations are no longer the all-powerful monopolists of the Progressive Era, but there is little doubt that business corporations are very influential.

In the late 1800s, corporations were the dominant, if not the only category of special interest. The main focus of the corporate owners, making maximum profits by monopolizing entire industries, was pretty clear to all. And even though the early corporations were very large, they were engaged in relatively few enterprises, and the enterprises themselves were fairly simple and employed straightforward, understandable processes. The corporations made steel, or dug coal, or operated railroads, or refined and distributed petroleum. Also, the financial markets these early corporations leveraged were rudimentary by today's standards.

Today, corporations are more complicated. They are engaged in many more types of business, and business processes are far more complex. Many are multi-national corporations. Many are tied together with strategic partnerships. There are still coal miners, steel makers and oil companies, but now there are also companies in a far wider range of industries, such as pharmaceuticals, automobiles, software, and companies providing national or international services, such as airlines, medical services, retail stores, even restaurants. The number of corporate special interests has grown as fast as the number of areas they are doing business in.

Another significant difference between Progressive Era special interests and those today is that there are many special interests that are not corporations in the traditional business sense. These include powerful and well-funded trade associations, owners associations, professional associations, teacher unions, labor unions, social advocacy groups, and environmentalist groups.

Public and private universities have become large, multi-function organizations engaged in activities far beyond educating students. Universities compete for billions of federal dollars to conduct research and to complete studies across a wide range of subjects. They are federally-funded to support numerous institutes and study centers which promote prescriptive policies for the government. These institutes employ hundreds of people and supply a continuous stream of "experts" to counsel congressional committees or to serve as executive branch appointees to bring their advocacy and expertise to government policy. University education is a full time ongoing enterprise that is closely tied to the federal government. It joins the growing host of special interests.

Non-profit institutions which are intent on promoting special interests have proliferated in recent decades. Most people think of non-profits as charitable and religious groups. Many are, and many state and local governments exempt them from paying taxes in order for these social-welfare groups to serve people in need. It is understandable that citizens equate non-profit with good works.

But many non-profit[8] organizations are primarily focused on policies and programs; they are what we know as activist groups. They raise funds for "outreach programs," "education" and "advocacy." In other words, they are essentially privately-funded enterprises whose business is to promote special policies or programs through the political process. Today, there are activist groups which specialize in all manner of subjects, including the environment, human and public health, civil liberties, gun control; the list is long and growing.

The number of special interest groups is large, and their areas of interest are broad and varied. Corporations are just one subset of the population of special interests. Yet, the conventional wisdom says corporate political spending is to blame for putting special interests above the general public. (I have included, parenthetically, the adjectives typically used to make the case.)

Corporations push favorable candidates with ("huge") campaign contributions and by ("pumping thousands of dollars toward") funding political action committees who advocate indirectly for their candidates. This ("undisclosed cash") gets the favored candidate elected. Once the candidate is in office, corporate lobbyists are granted ("unlimited") access to the elected official to push their ("greedy") agenda. Corporations continue spending ("gobs of") cash to provide officials with private jets, or to fund causes or charities favored by the official, or to provide ("lucrative") jobs to the official's family and friends. All the while, the corporations provide ("a steady stream of") campaign contributions for the official's reelection ("war-chest"). With ("all this") money, corporations buy what they want.

But the conventional wisdom is both overly simplistic and mostly wrong. The influence that special interests, corporate or otherwise exert is not the result of overt or covert corruption, or of excessive "money in politics", as implied by the conventional wisdom. The real reasons that special interests have tremendous influence are more complex, and should be more troubling to the average American than the conventional wisdom suggests.

Corporations and special interests are empowered because the federal government encourages their input and rewards them for being engaged in political decisions. The federal government's active involvement in so many areas is directly responsible for empowering corporate and special interests, and federal officials, elected and appointed, are complicit.

Because the federal government is regulating more and more activities and enterprises, it is a natural reaction for corporations and special interests to focus on what the federal government is doing, or intending to do. They expend resources to both stay informed and to try to influence outcomes such that their interests are, if not promoted, at least not harmed. They spend their money in ways that their cost-benefit analyses support. Almost all of them spend money legally; there are too many severe downsides to engaging in illegal activity.

The work of Congress is done in committees, supported by professional committee staff personnel who are hired because they have experience and expertise in particular subjects. Similarly, the work of the federal agencies and departments is done by federal employees or contract consultants who, again, have specific experience and expertise. Two facts of life intrude here that work to connect corporations and special interests to the federal government. First, although both Congressional and Executive-level professional staffers are capable people and are provided with reasonable resources and support to do their jobs, they often need input from outside. Almost always, corporations or non-profit enterprises employ the professionals who can provide additional expertise or insights. Congressional staff can invite corporate or non-profit employees to meet with them to solicit information or discuss the potential impact of new draft legislation. Federal executive-branch officials sometimes issue a formal Request for Information, seeking specific input and analysis from corporations and private enterprises, including non-profits. Second, government staff personnel with the requisite expertise have to come from somewhere. Many are recruited from the corporate world and engaged in the businesses which the government staff personnel are regulating. Federal and Congressional staff employees belong to professional organizations heavily populated with private sector experts; they attend conferences and trade shows with their corporation counterparts. In short, government experts are members in subject matter communities with strong corporate and non-profit representation.

The other arena in which corporations and non-profits connect with the federal government which encourages their influence is political appointees to the Executive Branch. The driver, again, is finding appointees with knowledge and management experience in specific subjects. Presidential administrations from both political parties draw from private sector corporations and from non-profit organizations. The Obama administration has drawn heavily from public and private universities. Earlier administrations drew mostly from a mix of for-profit and non-profit corporations, drawing from universities for foreign affairs experts.

Some contend that the close personal and professional associations between those inside government and those outside government create a condition ripe for corporations to exploit the federal government for corporate gain. Although I agree that the arrangement is potentially ripe, or at least fertile for such abuse, it is rare. There are (criminal) laws against it. There are regulations and rules, and institutional constructs which preclude it. And it overlooks an important guarantee against abuse: the character of most Americans, and especially Americans who volunteer for government service. Most of them are people of integrity and they are motivated to do what is best for their fellow Americans.

These relationships between corporations and the federal government are a practical reality. They do not, in and of themselves, predispose Congress, the Executive Branch or the federal bureaucracy to advance corporate interests over public interests. The public interest is promoted by having corporations that are healthy and competitive, which means profitable; they provide employment, foster communities, and provide a tax base.

The special interest landscape is very different than when Progressive Era reformers used government to tame monopoly corporations that were exploiting everyone. Back then, special interests did all they could to limit federal regulation and to prevent federal involvement in the economy. In contrast, today, most special interests encourage more federal regulation to advance their agendas and try to increase federal spending on specific things. Special interests can't simply pay-off politicians like the robber barons did. Instead they funnel money to support the campaigns of federal officials who advance their enterprise, and they devote substantial resources to lobbying and cultivating public opinion.

In some respects, corporations are the most restricted of today's special interests in terms of influencing the Congress in particular and the federal government in general. Corporations have clear objectives, they have known spheres of activity, and they are subject to fairly strict rules and regulations. As mentioned earlier, corporations must balance spending resources on political activities against their bottom lines. Of course, there are some highly profitable corporations that have more money available to spend on political activities. But the free market is unforgiving of corporations, even those with high profit margins; corporate executives and owners of private corporations don't indiscriminately spend money on political activity.

Beyond corporations, there are hundreds of non-profit enterprises that advance a wide range of special interests and that work to attract federal grants and contracts. Many of the non-profit enterprises are helpful. They can help policy-makers craft good rules, they can articulate the aspects of current problems, and they can provide feedback on existing programs and policies.

But non-profit activist groups can be more disruptive of good governance than helpful. The robber barons were destructive because they sought to monopolize industries. Some activist groups seek to monopolize political discourse. They seek to control or influence the flow of information, and use propaganda to influence voters or public opinion. They join or establish political action committees to influence political campaigns. Of course, all special interests use public relations and campaign contributions to try to promote their interests. Activist groups are comprised of people of one mind on a singular issue. Most non-profits, and most corporations, represent groups of people with varying opinions. They tend to advocate for some kind of activity or enterprise that is not usually political. Activist groups, on the other hand, advocate for specific governmental action.

Corporate and special interest money flows toward political power; it doesn't create it. Government has the one thing that no other group, association or enterprise, corporate or otherwise, possesses: the power to control everyone. Our federal government has assumed control over almost all economic activity, and over a host of other activities. It is no wonder why attracting the favor or influence of the federal government has become the no-holds-barred prize of corporations, special interests, and advocates of any issue. Because the federal government has become the one-stop-shop for every governmental activity, it attracts the greatest attention, and the concomitant resources of those affected by it. The brightest outdoor bulb attracts all the insects; the insects don't give the bulb its light.

In contrast to the powerful resources and influence of corporations and political non-profits, the average citizen and local communities have neither the resources nor the voice to reach federal representatives in a meaningful way. There are 435 members in the House of Representatives. On average, each member represents about 650,000 people. If a member spent half of every work day doing nothing except talking with constituents for six minutes each, the member would have input from about 15,000 people in a year. Constituents used to write letters to Congress; now they send thousands of emails or faxes. Most of the communication is dutifully filed and their views are compiled by Congressional staffers. The faxes and emails are usually related to a specific issue or pending piece of legislation. Often a host of constituents will flood a Representative's office with similar correspondence, usually in reaction to prodding by a special interest group seeking to sway votes on a specific piece of legislation. But in the aggregate, constituent input has marginal impact. (Your own Congressman or Senator will vehemently deny this, of course).

Local officials and even elected state government representatives have no more influence over the federal government than individual constituents, maybe even less. There are very few institutional or political connections between state and local officials and federal representatives. Even more importantly, there are no real mechanisms for coordinating state and federal legislation. Conflicting state and federal laws are sometimes resolved in the courts. There are no mechanisms to limit redundant or overlapping laws and regulations.

Special interests openly contribute to campaigns and political action committees for federal elections. Senators and Congressmen don't need to rely on state and local people to finance campaigns. They can pay private firms and consultants to manage campaigns, rather than having to engage with the electorate and develop a network of campaign volunteers.

Special interests influence Congressional committee staff and executive branch agencies. Most constituents have no idea the importance of staff personnel. Even if they did, most would have no idea who or where they are, or how to connect with them.

Constituents usually express their complaints or concerns in general terms. Lobbyists, on the other hand, possessed with intimate and expert knowledge on specific issues provide actionable information. Constituents usually ask their Congressman to do something or to try harder, sentiments that are difficult to distill into actionable steps.

Finally, the sheer number of lobbyists and the number of topics they cover distract members of Congress and their staff from examining district-wide or state-wide issues. As a result of special interest influence, constituent interests are simply drowned out by special interests.

The concentration of political power and regulatory control in the federal government is the reason that it is the center of attention and the focal point of special interests. Only by dispersing power away from the federal government and putting it closer to the people will public welfare, not corporate and interest group priorities again be served.

Agility

The Constitution's design for shared powers among the branches of the federal government is intended to provide a stable national government that preserves individual liberty by preventing the rise of tyranny. The Constitution's political structure makes introducing change a deliberately slow process and includes structural checks and balances to prevent concentration of political power.

The federal government enacts laws through legislation. Executive agencies initiate new programs, or adapt existing ones to comply with the legislation. Executive agencies also issue regulations to implement legislation. Crafting regulations requires extensive study, analysis and inter-agency review to ensure that regulations meet the letter and intent of new enabling legislation and comport with existing regulations. Generally, agencies craft programs and regulations to apply the law fairly, consistently and evenly across the entire national domain. In other words, one size fits all. It becomes technically complex and politically difficult if programs and regulations are tailored to local or regional conditions and characteristics.

It is a very long process, usually measured in years, from the time an issue is raised, legislation is enacted, and then federal regulations are crafted and published. Typically, a few isolated developments highlight an issue to start with. Or, in other cases, the way a state or local government mismanaged or failed to manage an issue is the basis for federal action. In either case, with little subject matter expertise and with limited understanding of the potential consequences that will result from new legislation that will affect fifty states, countless counties, and millions of people, the federal government issues its dictates.

In short, federal regulation of far-reaching topics is initiated in suspect ways. Regulations are created and promulgated very slowly, they are applied with a consistency that is oblivious to local differences, needs and conditions, let alone respectful of state or local law or community practices. And they frequently incur unexpected costs that are borne by state or local taxpayers.

Federal regulations are nearly immune from effective feedback. Implementation is overseen in a simplistic and legalistic way. Federal agents contrast the letter of various regulations with how people, organizations or companies apply the regulations. There is no consideration for how well the regulations are achieving their intended purpose. Even if there was such consideration, there is no mechanism for federal agents to suggest changes or improvements to the regulations. The only discretion that federal agents have is to sometimes overlook violations of regulations.

The main mechanism for challenging the enforcement of federal regulations, or the federal regulations themselves, is through the courts. Most often, this is ineffective because the courts decide the challenge on a legal basis, which means comparing the challenge with the language of the regulation. Or, the decision revolves around deciding between two seemingly conflicting regulations. In either case, the result is merely a judgment for or against a plaintiff; it does not generally result in changes to the regulations. Only when the lawsuit is predicated on the constitutionality of a regulation is there an opportunity for substantive feedback to change or modify the regulation. And this is rare.

If the federal government's deliberate and ponderous structure limits its agility, can reforms improve it? There have been numerous attempts to introduce reforms that improve the responsiveness, efficiency and effectiveness of federal government agencies. Most of the reforms are bureaucratic organizations or reorganizations. Most simply result in expanding the number of government personnel, creating new agencies or new divisions of existing agencies, or adding layers of rules intended to advance or streamline the government's work, but which usually have the opposite effect.

The federal government has proven capable of agile, effective and responsive governing - during major wars. But in times other than those of severe national emergency, the federal government is inefficient and slow. It is becoming increasingly inefficient as it adds layers of regulations and overlapping agencies. While the pace of change continually accelerates, whether in commerce and business, or communications, or in advancing technology, the federal government is less and less able to adapt. As companies are responding by working smarter, reducing overhead, and decentralizing operations, the federal government continues to expand, adds overhead and over-centralizes. Our country needs responsive and agile governance. Proper governance cannot rely primarily on a federal government that is increasingly ponderous and arthritic.

Deficits and Debt

The federal government is not constrained to match expenditures with revenues. It has expanded its activities and funded discretionary activities by issuing debt. It can operate with a deficit. It doesn't need cash reserves because it can borrow money or simply issue new money to cover years when expenditures exceed revenues.

All governments can take on debt. States and localities routinely issue bonds for projects. Localities use bonds to finance new schools and other capital expenses. States use bonds to build roads, bridges and state facilities. But there are significant differences between how states and localities manage expenditures and debt, and how the federal government does so. Most state and local governments restrict the use of debt to capital projects. Most further limit the total amount of debt that can exist, and many require a super majority or even a popular vote before debt can be issued. On the expenditure side, most states and localities require that, in each year's operating budget, expenditures cannot exceed expected revenues. In fact, most states and localities maintain a reserve fund from year to year, essentially a pool of surplus funds to guard against an off-year when revenues fall short of expectations, or to handle unexpected problems. None of these controls exist in any meaningful way in the federal government. Nothing requires the President's proposed budget or Congress's approved budget to limit expenditures to the amount of anticipated revenues. The federal government does not use debt only for capital projects. The federal government has a statutory debt limit, which would seem to serve as a cap on federal debt; but it is raised routinely by a simple majority vote.

Some Americans believe that the Constitution should be amended to mandate a balanced federal budget. In the 1980s, over thirty state legislatures approved petitions to convene a Constitutional Convention for the purpose of adding a budget Amendment. The number of states was a few states short of the necessary two-thirds of states the Constitution requires for a convention (but the petitions are still in effect and a convention could be called if a few more states approve a petition). A balanced budget Amendment may be necessary to force the federal government to reduce the debt and to limit deficits. However, a balanced budget Amendment is more a patch (and one that will probably be manipulated to diminish its effectiveness), and doesn't address the structural governmental systemic issues that bend the federal government to spend too much.

Persistent deficits are the result of the federal government doing too many things, politicians who have zero incentives to limit spending, and because a growing federal debt has thus far not had any significant downside.

We have had huge levels of debt in the past as a result of wars. Debt surged from $90M to $2.6B during the Civil War, from $5B to $27B during World War I, and from $49B to $260B during World War II.[9] These debt levels were about 35%, 35% and 120% as a percent of GDP, respectively. The federal debt in 2010 was about $13.5T, close to 100% of GDP. Each wage earner in the United States would have to pay around $140,000 to liquidate the 2010 debt[10]. The debt at the end of 2011 was $15.2T. Immediately following our major wars, the country fairly aggressively paid off a healthy portion of the debt. Today, instead, the debt continues to grow.

Servicing the public debt has not, historically, and even recently, been a problem. Many now believe, however, that the debt could cause a financial crisis for the United States if steps are not taken immediately to stop deficit spending and to start paying off the debt.

Interest rates are at historical lows. At an interest rate of 1%, servicing the national debt costs $150B a year; not much compared to total federal spending of $3.5T in 2010. But if interest rates jumped to 10%, debt service would consume $1.5T. Comparing this amount to total federal revenues of $2.2T in 2010, it is seen that debt service would consume almost 70% of annual federal revenues. (In August 2011, Greece, Ireland and Portugal were paying at or above 10% interest on their long term debt.)

Most believe that we won't face such a debt crisis next month, or even next year. But most agree that if the debt continues to grow, such a crisis is inevitable.

The debt and deficits are driven by over-spending, the result of a federal government that continues to expand its role and activities into ever more expensive areas.

Continuous Expansion

Over decades of expanding federal activity, while the two political parties alternated in power, the federal government has enacted sometimes bipolar policies and laws that layer atop one another in an ever-growing morass of laws and regulations. Large corporations have the manpower to wade through the morass and to compile those pieces of laws and regulations into a roadmap that only they understand, and which they navigate to their advantage. Non-profit interest groups similarly craft guidebooks comprised of selected segments of regulatory language and laws that, when bound together, make advocacy for their agenda seem to be the law of the land. This ability of corporations and non-profits to focus on and extract from the morass of regulations those segments that they can use to their advantage gives them unwarranted influence. No individual representative, Congressional committee or federal agency rivals the knowledge of the morass which corporations and non-profits possess. Armed with their unmatched understanding of existing laws and regulations, corporations and special interest groups engage scores of lobbyists who "educate" agency staffers and congressional aides on the existing state of laws and regulations on any given topic. Then they point out the deficiencies that need to be corrected, the areas that need clarification, and new developments that call for additional rules or new policy.

If the lobbying effort doesn't achieve legislative or regulatory success, corporations and special interests file lawsuits in federal court wherein they use their unmatched knowledge of essential elements of the federal code to overwhelm the limited resources, both in manpower and expertise, of government attorneys and bureaucrats, and force federal judges to reach a decision that usually favors the corporation or the special interest group. This grand game requires engaging thousands of lawyers on both sides at a high cost that aides neither productivity in business nor efficiency in government.

For laws and regulations already on the books, the dynamics described above propel the federal government to continually and increasingly expand the number and the scope of regulations.

There are no effective mechanisms or processes to review regulations, to assess their usefulness, or to evaluate their economic impact. They also have no shelf-life. They may be revised and expanded, but rarely are they terminated.

Finally, one other factor propels the federal government toward never-ending growth. Advances in technology create new industries, new economic activity, and sometimes generates new social issues. Many times these changes impact the existing regulatory scheme. Sometimes, issues arrive from these changes that cause one or more interest groups to seek new laws or regulations.

Today, Congress has the power and the ability to slow or even reverse the rate of growth in the federal government. Yet recent history has not been reassuring. And, as I have tried to explain, there are systematic pressures and political incentives for Congress and the President to encourage further growth.

Final (Tertiary) Effect

An oversized federal government has had a tertiary effect. It has restricted the ability of state and local governments to decide how and where to spend state and local revenues, and it has reduced the tax base available to states and localities to provide state and local services.

There is the principle that the best government is the government that is closest to the people. The principle is usually applied in terms of the responsiveness of legislative representatives to the electorate. It was described earlier how corporations and special interests are able to exert pressure on the Congress and the Executive Branch and ensure that the federal government is responsive to their agenda, while individuals or communities have limited resources to influence the federal government. Responsiveness of the government is measured by the laws which are passed and the policies which are enacted. There is another aspect of responsiveness that is just as important: the sensitivity of elected representatives to the electorate's tolerance for taxation, both the type of taxes and the tax rates.

The federal government is responsive to corporations and special interests in crafting the tax code and setting tax rates, because they have the resources to understand the tax code's intricacies. They can advocate for minor changes that benefit their interests. The general electorate, on the other hand, is overwhelmed by the federal tax code. The best the general population can do is public pressure for limits on tax rates.

At the state level, the tax scheme is far simpler and more transparent. Most state income tax codes simply use the federal tax code to establish taxable income, and then apply a state-specific set of tax rates and tax brackets. States have few special exemptions, deductions or credits in their codes. Some states, of course, have no income tax at all. (Folks in other states ask, "How can they do that?") States rely on sales taxes, various business taxes and some targeted excise taxes (e.g., cigarette and liquor taxes). Local taxes are even simpler. Real estate taxes are the main source of revenue. The more your home and land is worth (whether it's mortgaged or owned free and clear), the more real estate taxes you pay.

The electorate understands local taxes and mostly understands state taxes. Voters also know how to exert political pressure to influence tax rates. But the typical American sees the federal tax system as untouchable. The federal tax scheme and federal tax rates are essentially unresponsive to the taxpayers.

Local voters understand where their local tax dollars are spent. Voters can't see the same connection between state taxes and state spending, but representatives to state legislatures and governors clearly understand how the two connect in the budget line items that compile state finances. But in the federal government, there is no direct connection between taxes and revenues. Even worse, federal government financial reports don't identify what spending is financed by revenues, and what is financed by borrowing (deficits).

Against this backdrop, members of Congress respond to pressures for more spending and pressures to lower taxes by doing both, and printing money to fill the gap.

In fiscal year 2010, in billions of dollars, total local, state and federal spending was around $1,500B, $1,300B and $3,500B, respectively. Of the federal spending, over $500B was transferred to state and local governments. The following table shows spending for fiscal year 2010, deficits and debt at the three levels of government, and the tax revenues.

Fiscal Year 2010 Revenues and Expenditures

	Federal	Transfer	State	Local	Total
Expenditures	3,456	-543	1,315	1,570	5,790
Deficit Spending	1,294	-	0	0	
Debt	13,529	-	1,034	1,610	16,173

	Federal	Transfer	State + Local	Total
Revenues	2,162	-	2,342	4,504

Table Explanation[11]: The first row tabulates the money spent by the federal, state and local governments. Part of the federal expenditure is not direct spending; some federal spending is transferred to local and state governments. This is called "revenue sharing" (although it is probably more accurate to call it deficit-sharing). In the table, the $543B transferred from the federal government is included in the state and local expenditures. The debt row shows what money is owed by the three levels of government as of the end of the fiscal year. The bottom line shows combined tax revenues are about 4.5 Trillion. Total expenditures are the sum of local, state and federal, less the transfer from federal: 5.9 Trillion. The difference is 1.4 Trillion, or 1,400 Billion, or 1,400,000 Million. There are about 100 million wage-earners and money-makers in the United States. (Divide the deficit amount, $1,400,000 million by the 100 million people to calculate the individual cost). Each earner would need to provide $14,000 in 2010 to cover the gap between revenues and expenditures. Each wage earner would further need to provide about $140,000 to pay off the national debt. Also, these figures do not account for future liabilities, particularly the future cost of retirement pensions.

Federal politicians and policy-makers, echoed by the national media and national level pundits, talk only in terms of federal taxes: income tax rates and national payroll taxes (social security and Medicare/Medicaid). But most voters don't focus on federal taxes alone. From their view, they don't pay just federal taxes; they pay all of these taxes. In 2010, they actually paid slightly more in state and local taxes than in federal taxes.

The total annual local, state and federal tax revenues reveal the true cost of the American political system as it now exists. Two themes emerge from this data. First, state and local spending generally equals revenues; in other words, state and local governments don't incur deficits. Second, federal spending is not constrained by annual revenues, and in fact relies on significant deficit spending.

Examining the historical trends of local, state and federal taxing and spending helps to put today's level of taxation in context.

Tax Revenues as a Percent of Gross Domestic Product (GDP)
(Approximate)

	1950	2008
Local	4%	7%
State	4%	9%
Federal	18%	18%
Total	26%	34%

Even though federal tax revenues as a percent of GDP have not changed over these years, total taxes have increased substantially.

Expenditures as a Percent of Gross Domestic Product

	1950	2008
Local	4%	11%
State	4%	9%

As shown in the two tables above, in 2008 state tax revenues and state expenditures were about equal at 9% of GDP. Local tax revenues were around 7% of GDP, but local expenditures were around 11%. Local spending was 4% more than local tax revenue. But local governments don't run budget deficits, so what accounts for the difference? The difference is primarily the result of federal "revenue sharing:" transferring federal funds to local governments.

The three tables above highlight the unusual state of taxation and spending in the US system of governments. Over the span of fifty years, overall tax revenues have gone up, but federal tax revenues have been flat. Spending at all levels has gone up. At the state level the increase in spending has been met with an equivalent increase in tax revenues. But local spending now exceeds local tax revenues.

These trends illustrate that Congress has been avoiding the politically difficult decision to raise federal taxes. Further, Congress has been relying on deficit spending to fund expanding federal programs without regard for the capacity of the tax base to provide revenue. Congress has also developed the habit of delivering local services via revenue sharing by subsidizing local governments.

The taxpayers take the brunt of this federal scheme, of course. But it has had a debilitating impact on state governments. Much of the increase in state spending has been forced onto states by the federal government. State governments have had to raise state taxes in order to pay for federal mandates. So, again, Congress can take credit for the federal government doing more good for the public without having to take responsibility for finding the revenues.

The net effect of the present taxing and spending scheme, dominated by the federal government, has been to limit the ability of state and local governments to generate additional revenues from state and local sources to provide more or better services, to maintain public infrastructure, or to make new public improvements.

It also undermines representative governance when the taxes required to support governmental programs are not tied directly to the level of government which is mandating the programs.

State and local governments generally despise this arrangement. But they don't have the political power to confront the federal government.

The Overall Impact

I have outlined the primary, several secondary, and the tertiary impacts of federal governmental preeminence. Together, they reveal a federal government that is undermining the entire system of federated governance by assuming control of most local and state prerogatives. Together, they also explain why the federal government is incapable of restraining its impulses, and why it is becoming increasingly incapable of reforming itself.

With an overwhelmingly powerful federal government showing itself incapable of effective governance, it is causing Americans to lose confidence in all levels of government. In fact, most local and state governments still work pretty well in the United States. Their elected representatives decide on government's roles, responsibilities and functions, and then they determine how to meet their obligations with taxes that the electorate finds tolerable. They deliver governmental services in terms of what they can afford, driven by the people's willingness to be taxed. State and local representatives make political decisions on governmental priorities and then oversee how administrators execute programs and deliver services. Some states and municipalities have played fast and loose in accounting rules and are in real financial trouble. But most who did so in the past are now taking corrective action to restore fiscal health.

State and local governments also have incentives for fiscal discipline that the federal government lacks. Servicing any debt competes directly with funding for delivering services, which tends to limit the amount of debt. State and local officials are closer to their constituents and more attuned to the level of taxation the people are willing to accept. This is particularly true at the local level, where real property taxes are felt by every resident of the locality.

But the tentacles of the ailing federal government now reach so deeply and broadly into local and state governments, the federal government is creating a crisis in all levels of governance.

The Effect on Congress

Political science suggests many theories as to how Congress works and why members of Congress act as they do. The theories are insightful but none of them are provable. However, one theory that is consistently affirmed and which makes common sense is the idea that the main motivation of members of Congress is to get reelected. In what follows, the reader should keep this in mind.

Politicians try to deliver what their people want and to enact legislation that will promote the public good the people expect. Members of Congress won't get reelected if they fail to do this. Before considering how this works in Congress, consider how it works in state legislatures. State representatives learn of a problem that needs to be addressed, perhaps as a result of an article in a newspaper, or from a conversation with a constituent, or because an interest group raises an issue. The state representative evaluates the problem to find possible solutions. After settling on a set of solutions, the representative first decides if the state government has the authority to provide a solution. If it is clear that there is no state authority to provide a solution, the representative tells whoever is interested that no government action can be taken.

If government action is authorized, the next question becomes, is government action possible. The government may already have agencies or programs that can provide a solution within existing law. Or, the government may need to enact new law to provide a solution. The state representative contrasts the severity of the problem with the added cost of implementing a government solution. If the severity is compelling and the cost is justified, the next decision point is where to find the funds. They can come from existing revenues or from new revenues. The former would require taking funding from other programs or activities; the latter would require raising taxes. The representative assesses the mood of the majority in his district: does the problem affect enough of them that they might support a government solution, and would they be willing to pay more taxes or support reductions in other areas to pay for the action. Most representatives rely on their instincts to make this evaluation, instincts developed by frequently staying in touch with friends and supporters back home. Ultimately, a political decision is reached if a majority of all the state representatives share the same assessment. More often than not, the majority of representatives conclude that their electorates aren't willing to pay more taxes and don't want to reduce existing programs, so no new legislation is drafted.

The factors affecting a state representative's assessment include the following. State governments have clear constitutional boundaries to their authority. Many state constitutions set strict limits on what state governments can do, and what they cannot do. The U.S. Constitution also sets limits on state governments. State legislatures and governors must match revenues and expenditures in annual appropriations, and have strict caps on overall state and local debt.

Most of these factors are not considered when a member of Congress makes an assessment as to the propriety of federal government action.

First, there are few limits on the authority of Congress to enact legislation. As has been explained earlier, the Constitution has granted Congress unlimited authority over the economy, and everything related to the economy. The Constitution had clear limits two hundred years ago, but not today. When examining solutions to problems, a member of Congress doesn't even consider if Congress has the authority to consider any given solution. Some members nostalgically cling to clauses in the Constitution which they cite as limiting Congressional authority. But decades of precedents, either written in Court decisions or embodied in federal legislation refute the member's arguments. The authority of Congress to do something becomes a political debate about the propriety of taking action.

There is no connection between federal spending and federal taxing. With no real debt limit and no revenue cap on expenditures, members are not compelled to offset the cost of new legislation with taxes or reductions to existing programs.

The federal tax code is the final player affecting how members of Congress make assessments on new solutions. Members of Congress don't have to worry about raising taxes that will affect their constituents across the board. If raising revenues becomes necessary, Congress can do it in ways that won't affect a majority of voters, or in ways that are hidden in the catacombs of tax law.

Congress has no structural, systemic or fiscal limitations. In this unconstrained arena, every issue is decided by winning political control. Every issue becomes a contest between proponents and opponents for specific governmental action. For decades, these dynamics pressured both national political parties to do whatever they could to gain political control of Congress. This had the effect of polarizing the two national political parties as they fought to gain political control. It was an environment that encouraged partisan national politics. But, no matter which party was in the majority, there was no counterweight to incentives for Congress to grow the federal government.

Now, however, the expanding national debt has captured the attention of a growing portion of the electorate. Many of these voters are convinced that the President and sitting members of Congress simply don't realize that more debt will lead to a severe financial crisis and could bankrupt the country. These voters are also convinced that there is not time to waste; the trend toward more deficit spending must be reversed now. A majority of the House of Representatives now sense that they must address the concerns of this growing number of voters if they want to be reelected.

This is game-changing for Congress. The two parties are not vying for control of Congress so that either party can legislate at will and spend money on what they want. The Republican Party is not just competing against the Democratic Party. The Republican Party is competing against Congress itself as it tries to impose a limit on Congressional authority. The result is not the partisan divide of the past. The result is Congressional gridlock. It is the proverbial clash between an immovable object and an unstoppable force.

Even if the immediate gridlock in Congress is resolved by elections that give one party a significant majority, the systemic pressures for the federal government to continue to expand will inevitably lead to gridlock in the future. The federal government's systemic addiction to spending will ultimately hit a hard ceiling of financial physics.

OBSTACLES TO REFORM

The Progressive Era of the early 1900s was the result of significant changes in society which required new modes and organizations for governance. Whether it was an industrial revolution, or more an economic evolution, it was evident by the early 1900s that changes in governmental processes were necessary to contend with the shift from a farming and mercantile based society to an industrial-based economy. Additionally, the United States population had increased from about 8 million in 1800 to about 80 million by 1912, the same year that New Mexico and Arizona joined the union, increasing the number of states from the original 13 to 48. People were more mobile and change was more rapid. Corporations were accumulating wealth at unprecedented levels, and government seemed powerless to protect average citizens from the power and influence of corporate barons. The country had witnessed frequent economic turmoil and financial panics.

Today, after the first decade of the 21st century, America faces a population of over 300 million, a thoroughly changed economic basis, and a world with unprecedented globalization and an accelerating pace of change. And yet, for the most part, the American governmental system remains founded on the Progressive Era reforms enacted one hundred years ago. Americans face similar concerns to those cited by Theodore Roosevelt in his call for a New Nationalism in 1910[12], but in an entirely different context. It is time for significant reform.

Reform requires the approval of a significant majority of Americans. In the formative years of the Progressive Era of the early 1900s, it had become clear to a broad swath of the electorate that major reform was crucial for the government to fulfill its obligations to the people. Both the Republican and Democrat parties pushed for similar reforms (even though both parties had polarized minorities that advocated, on one hand, near-communism, and, on the other hand, maintaining the status quo). This broad, popular support resulted in rapid passage of the 16th and 17th Amendments in 1913, which authorized the income tax and required direct election of Senators. The 18th Amendment followed in 1919, initiating prohibition, and the 19th Amendment in 1920, giving the vote to women. New legislation brought the Federal Reserve System, the Interstate Commerce Commission, the Federal Trade Commission, and the Food and Drug Administration, all of which were popularly supported, not just as an expansion of the federal government, but as an appropriate expansion of government regulation in general over a nationalizing economy. In 1914, the Clayton Antitrust Act was enacted to give the federal government the power to be proactive in preventing monopolies and anti-competitive practices, and to limit corporate influence.

Today, unlike during the Progressive Era, it is populist groups and a growing number of weakly-partisan voters who are generating a base that could become broad enough to promote major governmental-wide reform. More and more local and state elected representatives are further broadening this base. The groundswell is starting to penetrate the Republican Party and segments of the Democratic Party.

There are two main obstacles to reform, one practical, one attitudinal. At the practical level, entrenched politicians, national political parties, and the powerful network of special interest advocates are heavily invested in maintaining an over-active federal government that centralizes all governance and spends without restraint. Attitudinally, a majority of voters will need to reject the ingrained orthodoxy that any problem anywhere in the nation must be addressed with a national-level solution coming from the federal government.

The former can only be overcome by pervasive popular pressure. The latter will require articulate leadership that can awaken people's minds to the realization that state governments are as capable as a federal government, if not more so, to provide effective social and community governance.

In the introduction, I touched on the issue of entrusting more governance to state governments. The American system of federated governments was founded on the concept of energetic, effective and competent state governments. In concluding this chapter, here follows more reasons why our states can be capable stewards of American governance.

Social scientists and opinion columnists frequently compare American laws and policies to those of other countries, the former to evaluate alternative policies, the latter to either extol or decry how Americans do things. Most of the time, they examine how the American federal government compares with the central government of other countries. But comparison with other countries can also be a way to gauge the capacity of states to govern. One assumption must be made: that the capacity of modern, economically advanced countries (or U.S. states) can use population as a basis for that capacity. I believe this is a valid assumption.

This next table contrasts the populations of countries often compared to the United States with the population of U.S. states (in millions of people).

Germany	82M
France	65M
UK	63M
Canada	34M
Australia	22M
Netherlands	17M
Portugal	11M
Belgium	10M
Sweden	9M
Switzerland	8M
Israel	7M
Denmark	6M
Finland	5M
New Zealand	4M

CA	37M
TX	25M
NY, FL	19M
IL, PA, OH	12M
MI, GA, NC	10M
NJ	9M
VA	8M
WA, MA, IN	7M
AZ, TN, MI, MD, WI	6M
MN, CO, AL, SC, LA	5M
KY, OR, OK, CT	4M

For direct comparison with the United States, it is even a stretch to say that the largest of the countries listed are a reasonable basis for comparison. Germany is often cited, even though it has about one-fourth the U.S. population, and 4% of the landmass. Combined, the populations of California and Texas are about the same as the United Kingdom or France; California alone has a larger population than Canada; Texas alone has more people than Australia. The bottom of the list is thought-provoking. These relatively small countries are recognized as major players in the world economy, as important contributors to global diplomatic initiatives, and as examples of good democratic governance. Almost thirty states have as many people as these smaller countries. Thirty-five U.S. states have 3 million citizens or more. Even the least populous state, Wyoming, has over 560,000 inhabitants, which is more than the 530,000 residents of Virginia in the 1780s, by far the most populous state at the time (total U.S. population then was under three million). Some of these smaller countries, even with relatively small populations, are quite capable of not just providing for their inhabitants, but also for regulating their financial systems, controlling immigration, and even providing military forces for their national security.

Israel's seven million people provide a government that does everything for its people. U.S. states don't have to do everything; they have the advantage of a federal government that can provide for common state interests. States are able to focus on their local and regional issues, on the health of their communities, and on the economic vitality of their society. Every U.S. state also has robust civil organizations and institutions to ease governance, including good universities. Each state also has its own Constitution, tailored for its specific climate, geography and economy; and states are not hesitant to change their Constitutions on a regular basis.

Importantly, there are many more elected Representatives to state legislatures than to the Congress. State representatives are much closer to the people of the state, and they are directly affected by many of the laws that they write, and how regulations from those laws are administered.

Of the larger countries listed in the table above, three have federal systems which are similar in many ways to the U.S. system. Australia has six states and three territories. Canada has ten provinces and three territories. Germany has sixteen states, ranging in population from 700,000 to almost 18 million. It is probably not a coincidence that in the post-2008 economic downturn and financial crises, these three countries with robust federal systems have managed to avoid the difficulties that have plagued advanced countries with more centralized governments. Germany's performance is particularly compelling in contrast to most of the rest of Europe.

America's history of state governance, the modern experience of other large countries with federal systems of governance, and the proven governing ability of small modern countries make a strong argument that each and every U.S. state has the capacity and the political systems to govern effectively and efficiently.

There is another point to stress about state governments. Many people think that the U.S. government is broken and is hopelessly grid-locked. They think that the Constitution, which spreads power among different branches and has various checks and balances, prevents the government from operating effectively, let alone efficiently, and that it prevents the government from enacting progressive, proactive or prudent policies to foster U.S. competitiveness or to provide for social needs. There is truth in this viewpoint. The Constitution intentionally limits the power of the Federal government to do things.

States are generally unrestrained in their power. States can write into their constitutions all sorts of authority for state or local governance. The only true restraint is what the U.S. Constitution says that states cannot do. Four states, Virginia, Massachusetts, Pennsylvania and Kentucky refer to themselves as Commonwealths. They exist to provide public commons to promote the public wealth as much as they exist to enforce the rights of their citizens and to assure their safety.

Some refer to states as laboratories of democracy. I think the phrase is trite. But it does capture the fact that states have far more latitude than the federal government to enact wide-ranging laws and to attempt imaginative programs to try to help their people and to improve their communities.

Countless federal laws mandating state and local rules have had a very broad chilling effect on states. State governments waste time and resources trying to comply with countless federal regulations instead of focusing on what their people need.

Today's American people need to enact reforms that match the American governmental system with the needs and expectations of its people in post-industrial and post-modern times.

Recommended Reforms

Is the federal government operating within its Constitutional limits today? Politicians and legal scholars have debated this question long and hard for years. Most often, the debate revolves around the laws which Congress enacts in executing the powers granted in Article I, Section 8, known as the enumerated powers. The Commerce clause, one of the enumerated powers, has been interpreted to give the federal government unlimited power to regulate economic matters, as described earlier.

But beyond Section 8 in Article I, the federal government is generally in full compliance with the Constitution's six Articles and twenty-seven Amendments. State governments are in full compliance as well. It is not often mentioned, but Section 10 of Article I prohibits states from exercising some power. As a result of the 14th Amendment and Supreme Court decisions, states are also required to be in compliance with most of the Bill of Rights, and provisions of other Amendments.[13]

The U.S. Constitution was written to establish a national government that would provide for the common defense, act to represent the states to foreign governments, and which had the power to make the states work together in commerce. The U.S. Constitution is but a part of the American system of governance. The document's primary purpose was to establish the structure of the federal government, and to specify how people were to be elected or appointed to federal positions. Years before the Constitution was even drafted, each of the thirteen states had already enacted state Constitutions. Most of these had specific stipulations on what powers state governments could and could not exercise. Most also had a Bill of Rights which was more extensive than what would become the first ten Amendments to the U.S. Constitution.

The question that started this chapter is interesting, but it is irrelevant. The real question, and the question begged by the first, is this: Does the Constitution define the proper role of the federal government today?

If the Constitution is vague, and requires legal interpretation to construe its meaning, why not remove the ambiguity and agree on clear language? This is precisely what the Founding Fathers did in the original text. As a group, they constructed the text with words which in their day combined to produce a system for governance that was clearly understood by all of them. The original Constitution was a new layer atop accepted and understood state Constitutions in a system of governance that would promote progress for all in the economic and social context of the day.

The day is well overdue to revise ambiguous, vague and outdated sections of the Constitution and to replace them with plain English. When the Constitution was first ratified, government debt was a reality. But it was assumed and expected that the debt from the Revolutionary War would be retired, and that the federal and state governments would spend just enough to provide for necessary government functions while servicing the debt. There were no Constitutional provisions for fiscal controls. Over the years, every state government has implemented statutory or Constitutional controls over taxing, spending and controlling levels of debt. Similar Constitutional controls for the federal government are needed.

When it was written and ratified, the Constitution meant what it said. Its words conveyed a clear meaning to all Americans at the time. Certainly, many compromises were made while crafting the Constitution and in finalizing the structure of the federal government and in deciding on the powers it would have. When the final draft was finished, its meaning was clearly understood. The words were deliberately chosen and the clauses carefully constructed. No ambiguous terms were used; no clauses were included which would require interpretation. Indeed, for a committee to reach consensus on a document which was formed through compromise, the language must clearly reflect, without ambiguity, what it says. The final text of the first ten Amendments was also unambiguous at the time.

Even though the original Constitution was written with clarity and supported by consensus, there were problems that quickly arose when the new Constitutional government was put into practice. Correcting these early problems was done expeditiously via Amendments. The 11th Amendment was ratified in February 1795, less than seven years after the Constitution was ratified. It added clarification that states could only be sued in state courts, not in federal courts. It was prompted by a 1793 Supreme Court decision. The 12th Amendment was ratified in June 1804. It required separate designation of presidential and vice presidential candidates, and provided more direction for electing them, as a result of the disputed presidential election of 1800.

The 11th and 12th Amendments demonstrated the willingness of citizens at the time to change the Constitution. The 11th Amendment was short; it was one sentence. The 12th Amendment was quite long, almost as long as Article III of the Constitution (which defined the federal judiciary). Like the Bill of Rights, these two Amendments were proposed and ratified in short order. The first ten Amendments were finalized in September 1789 and ratified by December 1791. The 11th Amendment was ratified within a year of being proposed, the 12th within seven months. The Americans who wrote and approved the Constitution were clearly quite comfortable with changing it, and doing so quickly, even in an age when transmitting information took weeks, not seconds.

After the 12th Amendment, the federal and state governments proceeded to govern for fifty years under a well-understood, Constitutionally-prescribed framework of federated governance. The end of the Civil War required modifying the Constitution. The 13th Amendment outlawed slavery throughout the United States, since President Lincoln's Emancipation Proclamation applied only to the states that had seceded. The famous 14th Amendment, ratified in 1868, was deemed necessary to prevent states from passing laws which discriminated against former slaves, and to prevent state-supported racism.[14] The 14th Amendment was also needed to correct Section 2, Article I of the Constitution, which had counted slaves as three-fifths of a person as the basis for tallying the number of people used to apportion the number of Representatives to Congress. The 15th Amendment was added in 1870 to prohibit states from denying any citizen's right to vote in any election. After this flurry of Amendments, it would be another forty years until the Progressive Era would provoke the next series of Amendments.

The Progressive Era was the last period that witnessed Amendments which made substantive changes to the Constitution. Amendments authorized the income tax, the direct election of Senators, and extended the vote to women. Since then, Amendments have made minor adjustments to the Constitution. Latter Amendments expanded voting rights, clarified the rules for Presidential incapacitation and Presidential succession, and limited the President to two terms. The last modern Amendment, the 26th Amendment lowering the voting age to eighteen, was ratified in 1971. (The 27th Amendment was ratified in 1992, but it had been proposed in 1789; it just took 200 years for the people to realize that it takes the power of the Constitution to prevent Congress from authorizing itself a pay raise.)

It has been forty years since the 26th Amendment was ratified. By comparison, in the roughly 200 years since ratification of the Constitution and ratification of the 26th Amendment, a new Amendment was added, on average, every 8 years. To look at Amendment history another way, sixty years separated the first twelve Amendments from those spawned by the Civil War, and then another fifty years until the Progressive Era Amendments. And it is now roughly 100 years since the substantive Amendments of the Progressive Era.

Today, there is general agreement that most of the Constitution means what it says. The structure of the federal government into three branches with a bicameral legislature, and the power of each of the branches with respect to each other are fully understood and generally inarguable. The Bill of Rights are clear, ingrained in the American system, and well understood (the 2nd Amendment, the right to bear arms, notwithstanding). Some aspects of the separation of powers between the state and federal governments remain as clear to people today as they were to the people of 1787.

But, in critical instances, the Constitution no longer says what it means. What was plain English, and what some words or clauses meant plainly to a reader in the 1780's, are not plain English today.

This is most evident in the text of the enumerated powers of Congress in Section 8, Article I, and in a number of the first ten Amendments. Some of the words that are key to understanding include, "commerce," "militia," "privileges and immunities," "bear" (as in arms - and even the word "arms"), "cruel and unusual," and the entire text of the 9th Amendment.

The English language is uniquely adaptable at maintaining meaning in an evolving world. Words change their meaning to reflect common understanding of the true message they convey, new words are added, and arcane words are replaced. This inherent adaptability of the language is fine and well for most matters. It is problematic when words and phrases from 200 years ago are locked into a governing document. It is no wonder that different people can read the Constitution, compare it with what the federal government is doing, and arrive at opposite conclusions as to whether or not the government is abiding by the Constitution. It is no mystery as to why so many Supreme Court decisions revolve around either the meaning of words or the intent of the authors of the words. The language of the Constitution didn't change from the time when Plessey v. Ferguson decided that separate but equal was Constitutional and Brown v. Board of Education decided it wasn't. Because the language in parts of the Constitution hasn't been updated to be generally understandable, we have left it to the Courts to resolve political matters, and we have allowed our elected officials to decide for themselves what powers they possess.

When it was first handwritten, the Constitution began with three super-sized letters: We the People. The writers didn't start with these three over-sized words to provide an artistic flourish to the document. These three words emphasize that it is the people that establish the government, not someone or something, and that the people themselves are perfectly capable of collectively writing down what they want. We, the people of today, need to resolve that it is time to once again collectively pick up the pen and rewrite our Constitution so that it says what we want it to mean.

We should not be afraid of doing this. Article V of the Constitution is, fortunately, still written in language that remains fully under-standable today. Amendments to the Constitution can be proposed by two-thirds of both houses of Congress, or by two-thirds of state legislatures authorizing a Convention for the purpose. All of the 27 Amendments were proposed by Congress. The conventional wis-dom is that a Convention authorized by state legislatures would be a disaster: that nothing would get done, that passions of the day would result in radical changes to the Constitution, or that other dire consequences would result. (Of course, it is no surprise that it has been members of Congress who foster this conventional wisdom.) And it should be noted, of course, that the Constitution itself was the product of a convention.[15] But the mechanism for proposing new Amendments is beside the point until there is broad popular support for what Amendments are needed.

As history reveals, Amendments can be effective, and they can be proposed and ratified quickly. And the requirement that three-fourths of state legislatures must agree to ratify Amendments pro-vides strong safeguards.

Rather than asking what was the original intent of the Constitu-tion, and how do we return to that intent, we the people need to ask how do we want to govern ourselves today. What do we want to preserve from the original system which successfully promoted personal freedom and general prosperity in the social and economic conditions at the time? The people of the Progressive Era made modifications to create a system of governance which maintained the original structure of the federal government, but gave it more power over business, knowing that in doing so, it would reduce state autonomy and increase the risk that government would have more potential to interfere with personal freedom and liberty. But they boldly pressed on.

Today, the Constitution remains the authoritative source for how the federal government is structured and how power is distributed among its branches. But, in today's advanced social-economic con-text, the document's enumeration of federal and state powers is gen-erally irrelevant.

We the people still have an instrument that says how the governmental system is structured. But we have essentially turned over to federal politicians to decide what things the federal government can do.

The reforms recommended here return to the people the power over what the federal and state governments can do. And, with the proposed budget Amendment, the people will set a hard debt ceiling and tell the federal government how to craft and execute a budget.

The Progressive Era reforms gave new power to the federal government. The reforms suggested here, with one exception, don't take away any power or authority from government. They transfer some power to state governments, and enumerate some powers to the federal government that it is already exercising (e.g., regulating the airways and the airwaves). The budget Amendment is the exception. It takes away from the federal government the power to set the level of national debt.

I suggest the following changes to the system of American governance. Some changes will require Amendments to the United States Constitution. Others will require state action or federal legislation.

In Appendix A I offer draft language for the Amendments described below.

Rewrite the Commerce Clause

As explained in a summary fashion earlier, the Commerce Clause in the Constitution is the source of Congress's authority to regulate every aspect of economic activity everywhere in the United States. The Commerce clause states:

The Congress shall have Power to regulate Commerce with foreign Nations, and among the several States, and with the Indian Tribes.

The Supreme Court has interpreted the words, "to regulate commerce among the states," in such a way that Congress now has all the governmental power to regulate everything which has an economic element. The federal government has the power to set wage and price controls, to mandate labels for foods and merchandise, even to tell homeowners what they can grow on their own land.[16]

This interpretation evolved over a number of Supreme Court decisions starting in the latter half of the 1800s and on into the mid-1900s. Most would agree that this reading of the commerce clause runs counter to what it was meant to accomplish in terms of balancing regulatory power between the federal government and the state governments.

The main concerns of the Founding Fathers with commerce was keeping the states from enacting laws, taxes and rules that would discourage interstate trade and the flow of goods, while also providing for a common, national set of rules in dealing with international trade. In today's parlance, the Commerce Clause was essentially a "Free-Trade Agreement" among the states. It was never imagined that the federal government would assume the power to regulate the production and pricing of commercial goods, or to regulate the flow of commerce inside state borders. The Founding Fathers expected governments to regulate economic activity to promote the general welfare, by, for example, local zoning, or setting safety regulations, or even subsidizing commercial activities that provided a general benefit. But this was to be done by the states; the federal government was only expected to ensure unfettered flow of commerce between states.

There is no reason that states can't effectively and competently regulate commercial activities today. National corporations would complain loudly, decrying the need to contend with fifty different set of rules. This argument has frequently fallen on sympathetic ears of federal officials and Congressmen. It has been an almost magical complaint because it works to the benefit of both the federal government and corporations. By setting a national standard that overrides state standards, the federal official has more power and control. The member of Congress gets the gratitude (and financial support) of the corporations affected by the standards. Most importantly, the corporation simplifies its operations. Instead of having to try to influence the regulatory schemes of fifty states, it can focus on one-stop-shopping at the federal government level.

The commerce clause should be revised. The words, "and among the several states" should be removed. Other words should be appended to the clause to specify that Congress has only the power to ensure the free-flow of goods and services between and among the states.

Rewrite the Tenth Amendment

One of the greatest enigmas of the American system of governance vis-à-vis the Constitution is how or why the federal government has bloated itself in view of the constraints imposed by the Tenth Amendment. Here is what it proscribes: The powers not delegated to the United States by the Constitution, nor prohibited by it to the states, are reserved to the states respectively, or to the people. The history of this Amendment is probably the penultimate example of the law of unintended consequences. Or, perhaps, it is the greatest example of writing laws based on common knowledge, instead of writing laws that include legal definitions of the terms involved, so that the law doesn't become open to the uncanny ability of lawyers to find ancillary meaning in what seem to be simple words and sentences.

(Probably the greatest mystery concerning the Bill of Rights is the Ninth Amendment. It states: "The powers not delegated to the United States by the Constitution shall not be construed to deny or disparage others retained by the people." It is almost as if, exhausted after writing and rewriting the Constitution and then drafting the Bill of Rights, the delegates turned over the final wording of the Bill of Rights to a copy editor who dutifully tried to collate the sentiments into something resembling the ten commandments; and then the copy editor himself became distracted after the first eight, and had his secretary, or his intern finish the other two.)[17]

The Tenth Amendment should be replaced with a new Amendment that explicitly states what we want. I suggest as a starting point the language which North Carolina recommended for this clause in the Bill of Rights. It reads, "That each state in the union shall, respectively, retain every power, jurisdiction and right, which is not by this constitution delegated to the Congress of the United States, or to the departments of the Federal Government." Virginia had recommended the identical language.

Add a Budget Amendment

The Constitution is silent on how the federal government should plan and execute a budget. I suspect that the founders assumed when it was ratified that the federal government would adopt budgeting and accounting processes similar to those of the state governments, or would come up with its own workable system. About the only budget guidance to be found in the Constitution is that any appropriation for the Army was to be "for no longer than two years." Congress was also tasked to provide and maintain a Navy (with no limit on appropriations, since it was understood at the time, as it is today, that building ships is a multi-year endeavor).

Most states have discovered that the best way to craft and execute budgets with fiscally sound controls is to separate the budget for day to day operations from the budget for infrastructure spending and big-ticket items. The former is most often referred to as the Operating Budget and the latter, the Capital Budget.

Most states require an Operating Budget that is balanced, wherein total projected spending is less than or equal to total projected revenues. After the budget is approved and the fiscal year begins, spending and revenues are tracked closely throughout the fiscal year. The state Governor or Department Officials have some latitude to modify spending if it appears that revenues are falling short of what was anticipated. Most Governors don't have the ability to exceed budgeted spending levels in the event that revenues are larger than expected. At the end of the fiscal year, most years there will be a surplus. States treat the surplus differently. States also insist that the state Treasury maintain a reserve of cash, sometimes giving it the obnoxious and confusing label of a "rainy day" fund. The reserve is not for any day, rainy or otherwise; it is a means to ensure fiscal solvency. In many instances, an annual surplus is transferred to the reserve fund.

Most states fund roads, buildings and other large purchases in a Capital Budget. A new highway, for example, is a high cost item during its construction, but then has little additional cost for the life of the highway. The states use long-term bonds to acquire the funds for construction, and then pay down the debt over many more years. Most states have laws that prescribe what kind of projects or purchases can be funded within the Capital Budget, and they also put limits on the total amount of debt that can be held.

This type of budgeting has served most states well and kept them on a sound financial footing. Most states also include annual payments for employee retirement and health care costs in the operating budget, forcing a realistic assessment of the potential costs for these areas in the future.

The Congress has no budget mechanism for tracking operating expenses separate from capital expenses, instead lumping both together in annual appropriations. This is a system that makes it very difficult to exercise fiscal discipline. It inhibits effective accounting schemes. It is easily manipulated by grouping spending according to government agencies rather than by government functions, or by recognizing that there are day-by-day expenses, and there are expenditures for capital equipment and projects. But most importantly, there is no means for separately trying to keep operating expenses within some level associated with available revenues, and there is no means for assuring that there is a level on debt, and that the debt is tied to prudent capital expenditures. The Congress has no way of preparing a budget that puts debt in perspective, nor that tries to equate operating needs to available revenues. It is a system that, lacking structure, promotes undisciplined fiscal controls. In short, it doesn't segregate cash flow from cash reserves, or investments from spending whims.

I do not believe that a balanced budget Amendment is necessary. First, it would not improve federal and Congressional budget development and budget execution processes and would not instill any fiscal discipline. It would simply put a cap on total spending (spending where and for what?), and it would be easy for Congress to find all sorts of accounting tricks and work-arounds that would make the budget cap meaningless.

I believe a finance Amendment would be more effective and much more transparent. It would have to have additional controls concerning Social Security. American's were sold on, and continue to support Social Security because almost everyone pays into it with an expectation of later getting paid back. Social Security has a unique revenue stream and a distinct expenditure basis, and it should be financially managed with rigid accounting methods in a separate account. The Constitution should mandate segregating Social Security revenues and expenditures in a way that prevents revenues from becoming just another fungible revenue stream for arbitrary federal spending. It might be necessary to address Medicare in a similar manner.

The changes described above can go a long way to reining in the abysmal financial and budget processes and practices of the federal government, all of which do nothing but spur deficit spending. The changes are more extensive than a relatively simple balanced budget Amendment. When it comes to controlling budgeting, specificity is critical. Strict and clear rules are necessary. Every state has learned this. It is time to make the Congress operate with adult guidelines.

Additions to Article I, Section 9

Article I, Section 9 prohibits the Congress from enacting various kinds of legislation. Over the years, Congress has become more and more involved in local and community affairs. It has done this with direct legislation, and by instituting practices that promote federal meddling. Two specific practices should be ended. The only means to end these practices is to prohibit Congress from engaging in them. Congress should be prohibited from transferring federal funds to state or local governments. Sending federal dollars to states and localities is a noxious practice that hides from the taxpayer the cost of public, governmental services. It merely serves to bolster the election prospects of incumbent federal officials. It usually also tends to redistribute dollars on a per-state, rather than a per-capita basis; essentially a transfer of funds from states with lots of people to states with fewer people. There is no good reason to pay for local and state activities with federal tax dollars, except in times of national emergency or natural disaster. There is no good reason to pay for local and state activities with federal dollars.

Congress should be prohibited from enacting tax credits and narrow exemptions as part of the federal tax code. They don't promote fiscal discipline and they hide the cost of federal governance. Federal tax laws should be confined to establishing taxing schemes that are sound and equitable, not embellished with give-backs, caveats and exceptions. Tax credits and exceptions are essentially subsidies, but they are seemingly given at no cost to the taxpayer.

Federal involvement in education is counterproductive. Congress should be prohibited from enacting laws or regulations concerning education (except in support of education of Americans overseas with the military or diplomatic missions).

Return Choosing Senators to State Legislatures

The founding fathers believed that by having Senators chosen by state legislatures, the Senate would be a strong advocate for state sovereignty and would mitigate the federal government's tendency to assume powers that were intended to be reserved to the states. This provision for Senators to be chosen by state Legislatures was widely supported. In examining the Constitution's basis for the Senate in Federalist Paper 62, its author (probably James Madison) wrote,

Among the various modes which might have been devised for constituting this branch of the government, that which has been proposed by the convention is probably the most congenial with the public opinion. It is recommended by the double advantage of favoring a select appointment, and of giving the State governments such an agency in the formation of the Federal government as must secure the authority of the former, and may form a convenient link between the two systems."[18]

In their resolutions ratifying the Constitution, two states went so far as to request that the Constitution be amended to allow state legislatures to recall Senators. Rhode Island wanted "that the State Legislatures have power to recall, when they think it expedient, their Federal senators, and to send others in their stead."[19] New York went further, "... that the Legislatures of the respective States may recall their Senators or either of them, and elect others in their stead, to serve the remainder of the time for which the Senators so recalled were appointed."[20]

During the 1800s, the idea of directly electing Senators grew. With a growing population, greater and faster means of communication, and with the onset of the populist movement in general, it was soon a popular and widely supported notion that the people themselves, not their state legislators, should choose Senators in general elections. At the time, there were cases of Senate appointees allegedly paying state legislators to vote for them, and other cases of alleged corruption among state legislators and federal Senators. There were also a few instances when state legislatures were deadlocked, leaving a few states without representation in the Senate for extended periods. Although the alleged corruption cases were rarely proved, and instances of deadlock were overblown, these issues provided more grist to the growing consensus to change the way Senators were put into office. As a result of popular pressure, the seventeenth Amendment to the Constitution was ratified in 1913.

It remains arguable even today whether or not this change resulted in Senators being closer to the people, or more representative of the people of a state. But it is obvious that this change severed any accountability of Senators to state legislatures, and removed any incentive for Senators to promote state-wide legislation or state-wide policy. The change was much more than a simple break of what Federalist Paper 62 had hoped would be a "convenient link" between the federal and state governments. It turned the Senate away from a state-oriented institution to one that existed to serve the personal political ambitions of Senators, and to focus the Senate on competing for power with the other branches of the federal government, for its own sake.

Finally, and counter-intuitively, it diluted the people's representation in the federal government. It essentially created a second house of representatives, with representation by state, not based on population. The people of seven states are represented by one Congressman and two Senators. The winner is Wyoming. Its 550K inhabitants have three representatives in the Congress; roughly one per 185K people. California exemplifies the losers. Its 37M inhabitants have 53 Congressmen and 2 Senators, a ratio of one federal representative for about 670K people. The point here is not that the federal representative system is unrepresentative of the U.S. population, because it's not. It was never intended to be. The point is that state interests no longer have any representation in the federal government. There is no representation for state sovereign initiatives to influence the federal governance.

I am recommending repealing the 17th Amendment and returning the Senate to the tethers of state legislatures. This fits with recommendations for state legislature reform, which follows later. The two are not necessarily correlated or mutually dependent; rescinding the 17th Amendment would, on its own, restore more balance to the federal government. But, in terms of making the American system of governance more robust, reform of state governments along with repealing the 17th Amendment would fundamentally invigorate the body politic.

OTHER RECOMMENDATIONS

Simplify Federal and state tax codes

Of the many descriptions and recommendations in this essay, this area can be handled tersely. The federal tax code is beyond encrusted; it is runaway cancer. It must be replaced. It should be restored to what it once was: a simple set of progressive tax brackets, with no exceptions or exclusions. Exemptions should be restored to those that were allowed under the code in 1918: one for single, one for married, and one for each dependent. The brackets and exemption levels should be set to accommodate national averages that define where we, as a society, set reasonable levels of subsistence versus affluence.

All tax credits should be abolished, including the earned income tax credit. Simply, tax law should be tax law, period. Every citizen should be able to clearly understand, who pays and how much they pay. It should not be polluted with policy and programs.

The numbers of people and groups yelling "yes, but" about ending their tax advantages will seem insurmountable. The only way to overcome them all is to entertain none of them.

Unicameral State Legislatures.

In the midst of the Great Depression, state governments across the country looked for ways to cut the cost of governing. A popular tool was to reduce the cost of the legislatures, specifically by cutting the number of elected representatives. The more radical reforms suggested disestablishing one of the state legislative bodies, and shifting from a bicameral to a unicameral legislature. In the midst of the economic downturn one state acted quickly and disestablished its bicameral legislature. Nebraska remains today the one state government with a unicameral legislature. In 1937, Nebraska combined its bicameral legislature to a single state Legislature, and gave representatives the title of Senator (probably a palliative to the representatives at the time, the loftier title of Senator being more salving to the ego of the officeholder than the title of Representative or Delegate[21]). Nebraska has been no worse (and probably much better) for the try. The depression economy took an upswing before other states were financially forced to cut costs by reducing the size of their legislatures. But the lesson of Nebraska is compelling.

The cost of government was significantly reduced. The number of legislators was reduced from 133 to 43, a nearly 70% reduction. The 1935 bicameral session cost $202,593. The 1937 session cost $103,445, while passing 22 more bills in 12 fewer days than the bicameral session two years before. Nebraska believes that its legislature is a great success.[22] It attributes much of that success to the fact that it is a nonpartisan legislature. Candidates don't run as Republicans or Democrats, and the Legislature is not organized, managed or controlled on a majority-party basis. Another reason for the success is improved legislative transparency and efficiency. In the bicameral legislature, a small closed-door conference committee decided the final version of each body's draft legislation. In the unicameral system, the debates and tradeoffs on the final version of legislation is done openly.

It is interesting to examine other federal systems of government around the world that have self-governing states. Canada's federal system doesn't give its Provinces the power that U.S states enjoy (e.g., the central Canadian government establishes criminal laws), but the Provinces have broad responsibilities. Each Canadian Province has a unicameral legislature. Australia's structure is similar to Canada's; one of Australia's six states, Queensland, has a unicameral legislature.

There are sixteen states in Germany's federal republic, varying in population from around 700,000 to almost 18 million.[23] The German Basic Law prescribes the powers delegated to the states and those reserved for the central government. At the federal level the German government is bicameral. The Bundestag is comprised of directly elected representatives. The second house, the Bundesrat, is comprised of members from state legislatures who perform double-duty, serving in both their state legislatures and in the Bundesrat. Further, the Bundesrat must approve all federal laws that add administrative costs to the states. And, as with states in Canada and Queensland in Australia, and the State of Nebraska, German states have unicameral legislatures.

Bicameral state legislatures are an inefficient, unwieldy and outmoded construct for state legislatures. The 1964 U.S. Supreme Court decision of Reynolds v. Sims declared that state legislative districts had to be drawn based on the number of voters, and that districts defined by geographical boundaries were unconstitutional. In colonial times, the early states established bicameral legislatures, primarily applying the concept that two legislative bodies would promote more deliberate and considerate legislation, and protect citizens from overzealous factions that could develop in a unicameral legislature. But with the decision in Reynolds v. Sims, state Senates were no longer regional representative bodies, but instead were essentially a dual legislative body. State Senates and General Assemblies differed only in the number of members and the length of their terms. Both upper and lower state houses represent the same people equally and with the same focus; they are essentially redundant.

The old saw is that two are company, but three are a crowd. Co-equal but separate legislative houses defy the rule; together they are a crowd. The only people who benefit from having two legislative houses are those elected to fill the seats. State governments have no incentive to adopt a unicameral legislature.[24] The only beneficiaries are the people of the state. Here, Nebraska's experience is again instructive. The drive to implement a unicameral legislature was a popular initiative. A citizen, George Norris, led the drive, and in doing so, according to Nebraska lore, Mr. Norris wore out two sets of tires while driving across the state to gather support.

In today's complex and fast-paced world, governments need to be agile and responsive. As with the best large corporations, they should also be lean and efficient. A unicameral legislature is inherently amenable to adopting these characteristics, whereas bicameral legislation processes are intentionally ponderous and limit decisiveness.

Even more importantly, state legislatures need to have a concentrated and effective political consensus to pursue state interests, focused on the needs of their citizens, against what has become a dominant federal government. A bicameral legislative system is not capable of competing.

Other than the realistic obstacle of getting today's state Senators to vote themselves out of a job, the other impediment to a unicameral legislature is traditional American political philosophy. Federalist Papers 62 and 63 reflect this traditional philosophy, and mirror the strong support which existed at the time for a second legislative body, specifically a Senate. At the time of the founding, all states had bicameral legislatures. Much of the conventional wisdom of the time was based on the lessons of ancient democratic governments, including Greek and Roman governments. The main arguments for a Senate were that a second legislative body, populated with representatives who would be motivated to adopt a longer view, would balance the need for stable government with a government that promoted liberty, and that a Senate would be the institution which would serve to be, as Madison wrote, "a defense to the people against their own temporary errors and delusions." Also, Madison explained that there are two main objects of government. The first is tending to immediate problems; the second is what we today would call long-range planning. A legislative body motivated by a short term election cycle, particularly one with a large number of members who individually could shed responsibility for the acts of others, was not a body which could provide effective long-range plans and policies whose benefits would not be immediate. The final argument was that the Senate would provide a more "immutable" government, and thereby give the government more standing in the international community.

The final argument is not compelling when applied to state governments, but the other arguments need to be addressed. Tensions remain in representative government between being responsive and being mindful of the long term. The need to guard against short-fused popular notions and emotional responses to events also remains. Both of these concerns are rooted in the concept of time, what is temporal versus what is long-term. In the 18th century, one or two years were a relatively short time in terms of the pace of events and the rate of change. A duration of two years, the typical state representative's time in office, is today a relatively long period of time. Today, some would probably consider six years, the duration of a typical Senate seat, to be such a long space of time that predictions as to what the future will hold at the end of the duration are always wrong. Today, a legislative body with a tenure of two years will face temporal issues most of which are measured in days, if not hours, of media coverage. Against today's rapidly changing events, a perspective based on the totality of decisions and actions over a two year period is a relatively long-term view.

Early state governments were law-making enterprises. Legislatures were in session for mere weeks each year. During that time they passed laws and approved budgets, and then representatives went home. Enacting laws was a relatively simple matter of promulgating them. Executing a budget was left to the Governor and a small cadre of assistants and accountants who kept the books, and who wrote and mailed the checks. There was no body of government that was inherently stable and resistant to change. Today, with the growth of government agencies and administrative bodies, many would argue that it is the government itself that is too immutable. Today's great bureaucracies may be too powerful, and too wasteful, and too many other negative things. However, they do present a compelling counterweight to legislative exuberance or executive over-reach. Modern state governments are now, structurally and practically more tempered and un-reactive. Government itself has become a buffer against temporary errors and public delusions. A second legislative branch is not needed. A second legislative branch is now counterproductive, since most would agree that a primary problem of government today is not its over-action, but rather its inaction. A second legislative body contributes to the latter.

Finally, there is the example of the State of Nebraska, and its eighty year-long experiment of governing successfully with a unicameral legislature.

The obvious recommendation is this: adopt the Nebraska model, tailored for each state's unique circumstances. Representative government needs to be directly representative of the voters without dual representation that mires itself in political gamesmanship, and it needs to be capable of governing, of making political decisions quickly, transparently and with proper deliberative practices.

As mentioned earlier, since it made the change to a unicameral legislature, Nebraska also mandated a legislature that was non-partisan. I believe this step should be adopted by other states. It of course doesn't remove party politics from all aspects of state governing, but it does improve the representative nature of the legislature, and of the government as a whole. Most importantly, by removing party-based control of the legislature, it mitigates against party-based gerrymandering of voting districts.

The Net Effect

Taken together, these reforms would shift governance of major societal and community affairs and local commerce away from the federal government. By bounding the definition of Commerce to exclude federal regulation of any economic act, the basis for expansive federal regulations would be curtailed, and many existing federal regulations would be overturned. The federal government would be forced to plan and execute its budgets with greater transparency and with more fiscal discipline. For the first time, federal budgets would need to segregate operating and capital expenses, hopefully in a way that would better define the benefits of incurring debt.

By returning the selection of Senators to state legislatures, state governments would again have influence on the federal government. This influence would help to limit federal power over the states, would reduce the number of federal unfunded mandates, and would encourage more harmony between state and federal governance (or, at least mitigate the potential for disharmony).

This shift in governance would pressure the federal government to reduce expenditures. By limiting federal involvement in general and by restricting federal regulation of intra-state Commerce, many federal agencies and programs, and their costs, would be terminated. Other agencies and programs, and their costs, would be scaled back. State governments would expand, and would need more revenues. States would pressure the federal government to reduce federal taxes in order that states could raise theirs. This would restore more fiscal discipline because states cannot incur deficits like the federal government can. Finally, there would be less duplication of effort by state and federal government agencies.

Unicameral state governments would become more streamlined and more responsive. They would be able to address a wider range of issues because the legislatures could spend more time making decisions than in working out compromises between two legislative bodies. Representatives would be more accountable since they couldn't point to a second legislative body as the reason for inaction or mistakes.

This is not a set of solutions that will lead to a system of governance that will forever balance active government with governance that preserves liberty and freedom. It is but an update to the Constitutional, federal system that was established over two hundred years ago by people who agreed on a system they expected would preserve core principles, while allowing political to-and-fro to work out the particulars. It is an update to a system which allows heated debate about how to achieve desired ends. And it more clearly delineates at which level of government the work should be done to achieve desired ends. It is an update for a government of, by and for the people.

If adopted, these reforms would substantively change American governance. But they wouldn't be a radical change in direction. The basic tensions between individual liberty and effective collective governance, representing the needs of the people, are as real today as they were over two hundred years ago. These reforms would shift the fulcrum to restore balance between the need for collective safety and security and the desire for liberty, fostered by strong communities.

A Look At The System After Reform

What would American governance look like after enacting these reforms? The changes would revolutionize the federal government. But other than introducing fiscal discipline and restraints on the federal government, American governance would retain its current scope. In contrast to today's concentration of governance in the federal government, the system would be more focused on the general welfare, less influenced by special interests, and generally more agile and responsive.

Significant governmental control would shift to state governments. The following are some of the significant shifts that would occur.

Regulating and funding education for all citizens would be entirely a state function. The federal government would be limited to providing education for citizens overseas, those sent there as dependents of personnel in the armed forces, government agencies and diplomatic missions.

States would assume control of most environmental regulation. The federal government would be empowered to only regulate industrial and agricultural air emissions and waterborne emissions that enter interstate waterways.

States would regulate most economic activity. The federal government would be limited to establishing uniform regulations to ensure the free-flow of goods, services and information between the states.

The federal government would be prohibited from establishing a corporation, or from nationalizing an industry. States would have no such restrictions. However, this would mean the end of government sponsored enterprises, such as Fannie Mae. (It wouldn't necessarily end federal support for National Public Radio, however.)

A revised Tenth Amendment would clearly say that the federal government can't usurp state authority unless allowed by the Constitution. It further prohibits the President or federal courts from defining new powers of the federal government. It would further prohibit the President or the federal courts to grant new rights to government, or to the people, which are not included in the Constitution. This revision would, for the first time since the ratification of the 11th Amendment, redefine the power of the Supreme Court.

The federal government would be prohibited from enacting tax credits, and would be required to grant no exceptions to tax rules.

The federal government would be prohibited from "revenue sharing." The federal government would be empowered to only transfer federal funds to states or other organizations except in time of national emergency or natural disaster, and when required by treaties.

The U.S. Senate would retain its current place in the federal government. But the political motivation of Senators would change dramatically. Even though the country had significant experience with Senators being chosen by state legislatures for over one hundred years, it is difficult to predict what will happen by reverting to this construct in today's environment. I believe it will reduce the redundancy between federal and state legislation and regulation, and will put real pressure on Senators to rein in federal spending and limit the tendency for the federal government to collect more power and authority.

It will take the money out of Senatorial elections. There won't be any general elections. The Senate today is called a "millionaire club" by some people because a majority of Senators are millionaires, and because millionaires can afford to finance a state-wide election campaign. Of course, there might still be some electioneering of the public in general and state representatives in particular, but Senators will more likely be chosen based on an individual's reputation and commitment to the state, not because they can attract campaign money or use their own. Senate candidates could seek to buy a seat by bribing state legislatures. The perception that this was a reality was a major reason the 17th Amendment was introduced in the first place. But, Governor Blagojevich notwithstanding, there are safeguards and incentives against bribery and corruption.

One of the most positive results will be to significantly curtail the influence of special interests. At the federal level, the federal government will no longer be in the business of regulating everything, so special interests will be forced to focus on state governments. This will dilute their resources, and their influence. At the state level, state governments don't have the ability to satisfy special interests through deficit spending. Special interest lobbyists will not only have to convince representatives of the benefit in supporting their efforts, they will also have to explain why public funds should be used and what revenues should be used.

Further, by limiting the federal government's ability to insert exemptions and credits in the tax code, special interest lobbyists will no longer be able to solicit special breaks. Of course, they can try to do this at the state level, and state governments would decide if they are willing to use the tax codes for special exceptions. But state fiscal realities inherently limit the ability of representatives to entertain special requests that will provide a benefit to a few but spread the costs to the many.

Perhaps the greatest benefit in pursuing these reforms is repowering the people with their governance. As a country, we have convinced ourselves that the Constitution is sacrosanct. Politicians, who benefit from the status quo and proponents for centralized federal power have successfully persuaded Americans to keep their hands off the Constitution. By joining the debate over these reforms, and hopefully seeing new, substantive Amendments to the Constitution ratified, the people will again view the Constitution like its founders did: as something they write, that they agree on, and that they change when appropriate.

Afterword

This work is exceptionally presumptuous. First, it is offering a cure for governance ills which have accrued over a century. Second, and most audaciously, it is suggesting a way for "average," or "moderate" Americans to come together in a popular effort to restore governance to themselves, their families, their friends, their neighbors—and even to their political opposites.

Yet, the American experience remains unique, vibrant, robust and courageous. It is engendered by a land and its resources that offer us the opportunity to be bold. Without federal government help (and in spite of what the federal government has been doing), the United States is now exporting more gasoline and diesel fuel than it imports. The United States has extensive farmlands with the right combination of soil, sunshine, rain and climate that give the United States agricultural independence. Our vast country has numerous navigable rivers, great lakes and abundant natural seaports. It is a sublime combination of resourceful people and resource-filled territories. Its people have institutionalized fair laws and courts that give an honest hearing for the average to prevail over the wealthy and the privileged. It provides free public education for all, has a unique network of community colleges, and the best universities in the world. The United States have exceptional advantages and matchless potential.

It is a trite saying, that those who don't know the lessons of history are bound to repeat it. That is a chronological perspective. But there is also a geographical perspective. Those who don't know societies around the world have little perspective for gauging their own. Poverty in the United States is exceedingly rare when contrasted with poverty in much of the world. The pursuit of justice for all is robust in the United States; there is no system of justice for many people elsewhere. The pursuit of happiness is but an imaginary dream for most humans around the world, where survival is the general pursuit. This litany of comparisons is not to divert attention away from real problems we face in America. It is only meant to remind us that, as imperfect as the United States remains, American governance has been a framework that started with a war-weary, debt-ridden nation of three million and grew it to become what we are today.

In America, we have already decided that the individual has pre-eminence over the government; we just haven't perfected a system that assures individual preeminence while also empowering governments at the federal, state and local level to promote justice, the general welfare and security. We should keep on trying. We the People must be the ones to renew our great experiment in self-governing.

*   *   *

To aid the reader, the book includes the text of the U.S. Constitution in Appendix B. The Federalist Papers are a well-known source for understanding the Constitution. Another source for gleaning the intent of Constitutional text is each original state's Resolution for Ratification of the Constitution. These are included in Appendix C. It is fascinating to see what the states believed the Constitution meant, and what they expected to be included in the Bill of Rights. Finally, Appendix D includes the Bill of Rights in selected state Constitutions as they existed when the U.S. Constitution was written.

Appendix A:
Suggested Constitutional
Amendment Language

Revised Commerce Clause Amendment.

Section 1. The Congress shall have Power to regulate commerce with foreign nations and with the Indian Tribes.
Section 2. The Congress shall have the Power to establish uniform regulations to ensure the free-flow of goods, services and information among and between the states, territories and possessions; to exercise exclusive legislation over the airways, the airwaves, and interstate waterways; to regulate industrial airborne emissions and waterborne emissions that enter interstate waterways.
Section 3. That Congress shall erect no Company or Corporation engaged in Commerce.

As explained earlier, the Commerce clause has been interpreted by the Supreme Court to essentially grant Congress the power to regulate any aspect of economic activity. This is because the Court relies on the legal definition of the word commerce, not based on a Constitutional definition (because there is no Constitutional definition of commerce). Those who wrote and ratified the Constitution had a clear understanding that the power to regulate commerce among the states meant the power to regulate the flow of goods between states. They were concerned that states would disrupt the economy by enacting laws regulating imports and exports, or that states would levy tariffs against goods from other states. At the time, there was little economic activity based on the sale of services.

The new Commerce Clause was rarely discussed in the Federalist Papers. As James Madison wrote in Federalist Paper 45, "The regulation of commerce, it is true, is a new power; but that seems to be an addition few oppose and from which no apprehensions are entertained."

In their resolutions ratifying the Constitution, Virginia and North Carolina sought an Amendment which read, "That no navigation law, or law regulating Commerce shall be passed without the consent of two thirds of the Members present in both Houses." This confirms the common understanding at the time that regulating commerce meant regulating the flow of goods between states, and that such regulation could have a significant impact on the ability of state residents to freely move their goods outside of the state, or on the rivers and high seas.

The first two sections of the proposed is meant to give a Constitutional definition of Commerce, and what economic activity the federal Government is able to regulate, by clearly stating that federal regulation is limited to ensuring that goods and services flow freely, and without state impediment, between and among the states.

The third section is not this author's idea. The resolutions for ratification of the Constitution from New Hampshire, Rhode Island, North Carolina and Massachusetts contained an identically worded recommended Amendment, which read, "That Congress shall erect no Company of Merchants with exclusive advantages of Commerce." New York recommended a similarly worded Amendment. The early founders were probably beginning to examine the exceptionally generously worded Commerce Clause, and were concerned that it might provide an opening for Congress to set up its own companies, such as shipping companies or others.

Limited Power Amendment (to replace the Tenth Amendment)

THAT each state in the union shall, respectively, retain every power, jurisdiction and right, which is not by this Constitution delegated to the Congress of the United States, or to the departments of the Federal Government; that the President shall not issue any order or regulation except as necessary for the administration of Federal Departments; that the Supreme Court or

its lower Courts may render no opinion which has the effect of granting a power or right to the Federal Government which is not by this Constitution delegated to it.

The first portion is what the North Carolina and Virginia Resolutions on the Ratification of the Constitution (1789 and 1788) proposed for the language which ultimately became the condensed Tenth Amendment. The additional language is from this author.

Like the Commerce Clause, the Tenth Amendment was a general statement of limited powers which was perfectly understood by the founders at the time. There is little doubt that they ever envisioned legal interpretations of the Commerce Clause that would essentially strip the Tenth Amendment of its obvious and clearly stated intent.

The draft language above intends to be a more clear statement of the limits to federal power. Because we have learned that it is not just the Congress that is capable of assuming power, it seems prudent to limit the ability of the President and the Supreme Court to assume power not authorized by the Constitution.

The Tenth Amendment was an elegant condensation and compilation of the various Amendments proposed by the states in their resolutions for ratification of the Constitution. It is insightful to see what language some of the states recommended for what would become the Tenth Amendment.

New Hampshire: "First That it be Explicitly declared that all Powers not expressly and particularly Delegated by the aforesaid Constitution are reserved to the several states to be, by them Exercised."

Rhode Island: "First The United States shall guarantee to each State its sovereignty, freedom and independence, and every power, jurisdiction and right, which is not by the Constitution expressly delegated to the United States."

Virginia: "First, That each state in the Union shall respectively retain every power, jurisdiction and right which is not by the Constitution delegated to the Congress of the United States or to the departments of the Federal Government."

North Carolina: "I. That each state in the union shall, respectively, retain every power, jurisdiction and right, which is not by this constitution delegated to the Congress of the United States, or to the departments of the federal Government." (North Carolina and Virginia seemed more prescient than the other states by including federal departments.)

Massachusetts: "First, That it be explicitly declared that all Powers not expressly delegated by the aforesaid Constitution are reserved to the several States to be by them exercised."

New York (not a recommended Amendment, but included as part of the Resolution): "That the Powers of Government may be reassumed by the People, whensoever it shall become necessary to their Happiness; that every Power, Jurisdiction and right, which is not by the said Constitution clearly delegated to the Congress of the United States, or the departments of the Government thereof, remains to the People of the several States, or to their respective State Governments to whom they may have granted the same; And thos Clauses in the said Constitution, which declar, that Congress shall not have or exercise certain Powers, do not imply that Congress is entitled to any Powers not given by the said Constitution; but such Clauses are to be construed either as exceptions to certain specified powers, or as inserted merely for greater Caution."

Finance Amendment:

Section 1. The United States Budget shall include an Operating Budget, a Capital Budget, and Special Budgets for specific activities whose revenues are derived from specific sources.
(a) The Operating Budget shall include all revenues, less those included in Special Budgets, and shall include all expenditures less those included in the Capital Budget and in any Special Budgets.
(b) The Capital Budget shall include expenditures for all projects and programs funded by debt.
(c) Special Budgets shall include all revenues and expenditures for the particular project or program.

Section 2. Annually, at the times set by law, the President shall submit to the House of Representatives:

(a) A balanced Operating Budget for the ensuing fiscal year setting forth in detail (i) proposed expenditures classified by department or agency and by program and (ii) estimated revenues from all sources. If estimated revenues and available surplus are less than proposed expenditures, the President shall recommend specific additional sources of revenue sufficient to pay the deficiency and the estimated revenue to be derived from each source;

(b) A Capital Budget for the ensuing fiscal year setting forth in detail proposed expenditures to be financed from the proceeds of obligations of the Federal government or from operating funds;

(c) Such Special Budgets for the ensuing fiscal year setting forth in detail proposed expenditures and estimated revenues for the particular project or program; and

(d) A financial plan for not less than the next succeeding five fiscal years, which plan shall include for each such fiscal year:

(i) Projected operating expenditures classified by department or agency and by program, in reasonable detail, and estimated revenues, by major categories, from existing and additional sources, and

(ii) Projected expenditures for capital projects specifically itemized by purpose, and the proposed sources of financing each.

(iii) Projected expenditures and revenues for any Special program or project.

Section 3. Budgets and Appropriations.

(a) The Congress shall approve an Operating Budget, a Capital Budget, and any Special Budgets. Funds for servicing outstanding debt shall be included in the Operating budget. If the Congress fails to approve these budgets within two months before the start of the fiscal year, the budgets submitted by the President shall become law.

(b) Operating Budget appropriations made by the Congress

shall not exceed the estimated revenues in addition to any surplus available in the same fiscal year.

(c) The Capital Budget appropriations shall not exceed 50% of
the total Operating Budget appropriations.

(d) Outstanding debt shall not exceed five times the prior year's
Federal revenues, not including revenues for Special programs
and projects.

(e) All surplus of revenues over expenditures at the end of the
fiscal year shall be applied to the principal of any outstanding
debt, or, if there be no debt, shall be appropriated during the
ensuing fiscal year by the Congress.

Section 4. Revenues exceeding expenditures for Special Budgets
shall be held in a separate reserve fund and any fund balances
shall not be used for any purpose other than those directly related to the Special program or project, nor shall any fund balances
be borrowed or used as collateral for any other expenditures.

Section 5. The fiscal year shall begin on the first of October, and
end on the last day of September in the following year.

Section 6. This article shall take effect at the start of the next
fiscal year following ratification, except the debt limit of Section
3(d) shall take effect at the start of the fifth fiscal year following
ratification.

The above is a modified version of existing Virginia budget rules.
This proposed Amendment is not a balanced budget Amendment.
However, it would require a balanced operating budget, and it would
have a Constitutional limit on overall debt.

Rather than trying to specify what constitutes a capital expenditure versus an operating expenditure, or by trying to delineate what
things are capital purchases (like business tax codes), it simply requires that all expenditures funded by debt be accounted for in a
"Capital Budget," which could just as easily be labeled a "Debt
Budget." Nothing technically would prevent the President or Con-

gress from including any kind of expenditure in the Capital Budget. Congress could include an expenditure to buy food baskets to give away to federal employees. But, because the Capital budget is essentially a tool for clearly and transparently showing what is being paid for with debt, it is reasonable to expect that it will be the budget for major projects, war funding, natural disaster relief, aircraft carriers and the like. Of course, it could also include programs, such as unemployment benefits during recessions.

Social Security and Medicare would be Special budgets because they are funded by payroll taxes. The highway "trust fund" could be a special budget as well. In fact, the Amendment is written to require a Special budget for programs funded by specific taxes. It may be that the language needs to be more specific. The Amendment may need to say explicitly that Social Security must be in a Special Budget, or that all gasoline tax revenues must be in a Special budget.

Most state constitutions and statutes include detailed, even tedious descriptions of how budgets must be formulated, and how state governments must manage revenues, expenditures, and spending on capital projects, and set rigid limits on levels of state and local debt. States must do this because they don't have the ability to make monetary policy. It's not correct that states can't have budget deficits or debt; but states can't use monetary policy to manage their debt.

The level of detail in state rules is probably not necessary. But, Constitutional ceilings on the level of Capital budget appropriations in any one year (maximum of 50% of Operating budget appropriations) and on total debt (maximum of five times the total general revenues in the previous year) would provide real boundaries which should force fiscal discipline. It would be expected that Congress would write laws that provide more detailed budget rules.

Senator Amendment

Section 1. The seventeenth article of Amendment to the Constitution of the United States is hereby repealed.
Section 2. If Senate vacancies happen by resignation, or other-

wise, the affected state legislature shall be convened and shall choose a Senator to complete the term vacated with all due haste.

Section 3. This Amendment shall not be so construed as to affect the election or term of any Senator chosen before it becomes valid as part of the Constitution.

The Seventeenth Amendment to the Constitution did more than change how U.S. Senators were chosen. It also changed how a Senator vacancy would be handled. But the latter changes were necessitated by shifting the authority for choosing Senators from state legislatures to the voters of the state.

The second section would address one of the issues that the Amendment was meant to correct: legislative deadlock on choosing Senators. It would also avoid the issue of how to fill vacancies when the state legislature is in recess, and prevent a repetition of the recent fiasco associated with filling Senator Obama's vacancy.

The third section would keep existing Senators in place at the time the Amendment went into effect. It would maintain continuity. Also, it is probably needed to ensure that today's Senators don't create a political firestorm aimed at killing passage of the Amendment.

The general language of Section 1 is borrowed from the twenty-first Amendment, which ended prohibition. The language of Section 2 is from the seventeenth Amendment.

Additions to Section 9, Article I Amendment

Section 1. Congress shall transfer no Federal funds to any State or Territory, or to any government subordinate to any State or Territorial government, or to any one organization or corporation, except pursuant to treaties, or in time of national emergency or in response to natural disaster.

Section 2. Congress shall pass no law that authorizes tax credits, or otherwise authorizes specific exceptions to the general rules for the collection of revenues.

Section 3. Congress shall pass no law concerning education, ex-

cept as necessary for the support of the armed forces and of diplomatic missions.

In relative terms, these three sections are simple, but they would significantly redefine what Congress cannot do. First, it would get the federal government out of the business of sending money to states except in times of national emergency or in response to natural disaster. Of course, the federal government would retain the ability to define what constitutes a national emergency and a national disaster. But the words have pretty clear meaning to the general public and to politicians, so the political decision would be accompanied by common-sense debate, rather than legal interpretation. This section would end "revenue-sharing," the fairly recent practice of subsidizing state programs with federal dollars. Importantly, this wording does not impact the federal government's ability to distribute funds directly to individuals. It would not impact Social Security or Medicare. It would, however, prohibit the current Medicaid (and SCHIP) state-federal partnership arrangement, whereby states administer Medicaid and the federal government supplies matching funds to the states, and provides general guidelines and regulations. The current arrangement is fundamentally inconsistent with federated governance. Although moving responsibility for Medicaid to the federal government (which is what would have to happen) is inconsistent with the general theme of devolving more power to state governments, it is a reasonable exception. The people of the United states believe that government should provide the social support of Social Security, Medicare and Medicaid. Or, more accurately, the people want to provide a proverbial safety-net that keeps seniors out of poverty and provides medical care for the poor. It makes sense that administration of such a system should be done by the federal government, both because it has traditionally been doing so, and because it would be problematic if each state established and administered different programs. The national decision to permit redistribution of money from some citizens to others is best done with national consistency in order to prevent discrepancies between state programs which would most likely result in large numbers of people constantly moving from state to state to optimize their benefits.

Section 2 would outlaw tax credits and force federal tax laws to be applied evenly. Tax credits are nothing more than hidden subsidies. Section 1 of this Amendment would not prevent the federal government from sending funds to groups of organizations or corporations as a way of subsidizing an area that Congress decides would promote the general interest.

Section 3 would end federal involvement in education. Every state already mandates free public education, and states and localities pay for it. state education administrators need more authority to manage and improve education without having to waste time and energy overseeing federal rules and regulations.

Other Overdue Constitutional Updates

I will not suggest specific Amendments, but if we the people would agree to update the language of the Constitution, it would be a good time to identify clearly outdated portions and to consider some additions to address areas that the founders could never have anticipated. I am sure that there are other areas that should be added to this list.

The Second Amendment should probably be reconsidered for rewording to clarify the "well regulated militia" preface, despite recent Supreme Court rulings. There are many Americans who believe that it may also be time to limit the right to bear arms in some instances, and that some types of arms should not be included in the right. As written and interpreted by the Supreme Court, it seems that Americans have the right to carry a Stinger missile launcher around the neighborhood.

The Fourth Amendment gives people the right to be secure in their persons and houses against unreasonable searches and seizures. People nearly live in their automobiles these days. Also, the term house should probably be changed to residence. Some modifications are needed.

The Sixth Amendment assigns the right to a speedy and public trial. Courts have conveniently interpreted speedy differently than most people would understand the term speedy. It sometimes takes months or years for cases to go to trial. The Amendment should replace speedy with a specific length of time.

The Seventh Amendment sets the right to a trial by jury where the value in controversy exceeds twenty dollars. This Amendment should be modified and the dollar amount limit increased and tied to some other monetary basis so the limit can rise with inflation.

The Eighth Amendment outlaws "cruel and unusual" punishment. The Amendment should be expanded to include either punishments that are allowed, or punishments that are prohibited, or both.

The Fourteenth Amendment has been interpreted to mean things that increasing numbers of people are questioning. First, it says that all persons born in the United States and subject to its jurisdiction are citizens. The wording should be clarified to address those born of people who are not in the United States legally. Second, the Amendment prohibits states from making laws which abridge the privileges or immunities of citizens. The term "privileges or immunities" was probably understood to mean specific things when the Fourteenth Amendment was written after the Civil War; the term's meaning is not a clear statement today. The Amendment should be revised to clearly state those rights or freedoms that states are prohibited from outlawing.

An Amendment should be written which gives the Congress or the President powers that were certainly unanticipated in the 18th Century. Congress should have the power to regulate air traffic and the air traffic control system, to regulate the wireless communication spectrum and wireless communication standards, and to regulate industrial emissions which affect two or more states. The President should be given the power to direct offensive or defensive military action when American interests are threatened and there is no opportunity for a formal Congressional declaration of war.

Finally, consideration should be given to an Amendment which defines the authority of the federal government over territories, and the authority of territorial governments over themselves. The Australian and Canadian Constitutions address Territories separate from states, and could be a model on which to build.

One Final Consideration - an Apportionment Amendment

Here is part of the Virginia Constitution on apportionment:

Members of the House of Representatives of the United States and members of the Senate and of the House of Delegates of the General Assembly shall be elected from electoral districts established by the General Assembly. Every electoral district shall be composed of contiguous and compact territory and shall be so constituted as to give, as nearly as is practicable, representation in proportion to the population of the district.

Here is part of the California Constitution on apportionment, including changes required by the recently approved Proposition 20:

> In the year following the year in which the national census is taken under the direction of Congress at the beginning of each decade, the Citizens Redistricting Commission described in Section 2 shall adjust the boundary lines of the congressional, State Senatorial, Assembly, and Board of Equalization districts (also known as "redistricting")in conformance with the following standards and process set forth in Section 2.
>
> (1) Districts shall comply with the United States Constitution. Congressional districts shall achieve population equality as nearly as is practicable, and Senatorial, Assembly, and State Board of Equalization districts shall have reasonably equal population with other districts for the same office, except where deviation is required to comply with the federal Voting Rights Act or allowable by law.
> (2) Districts shall comply with the federal Voting Rights Act (42 U.S.C. Sec. 1971 and following).
> (3) Districts shall be geographically contiguous.
> (4) The geographic integrity of any city, county, city and county, local neighborhood, or local community of interest shall be respected in a manner that minimizes their division to the extent possible without violating the requirements of any of the preceding subdivisions. A community of interest

is a contiguous population which shares common social and economic interests that should be included within a single district for purposes of its effective and fair representation. Examples of such shared interests are those common to an urban area, a rural area, an industrial area, or an agricultural area, and those common to areas in which the people share similar living standards, use the same transportation facilities, have similar work opportunities, or have access to the same media of communication relevant to the election process. Communities of interest shall not include relationships with political parties, incumbents, or political candidates.

(5) To the extent practicable, and where this does not conflict with the criteria above, districts shall be drawn to encourage geographical compactness such that nearby areas of population are not bypassed for more distant population.

(6) To the extent practicable, and where this does not conflict with the criteria above, each Senate district shall be comprised of two whole, complete, and adjacent Assembly districts, and each Board of Equalization district shall be comprised of 10 whole, complete, and adjacent Senate districts.

These two examples highlight the key differences in how states set the boundaries for representatives' districts. One aspect is who decides how to set district boundaries. Virginia gives this authority to the state legislature. California established a Citizen's Commission. A second key aspect is how the districts are determined. Virginia requires that districts be defined primarily by geographic boundaries that seek to include equal numbers of people. California requires that districts also include equal numbers of people, but that they also comprise contiguous populations which share common social and economic interests.

There are two issues which drive these approaches. One is the practice of establishing districts that will give an incumbent or a particular political party advantage in winning elections. This is commonly known as gerrymandering. The second issue is establishing districts that will most likely elect representatives of specific groups. In California, the groups are defined as people with common social and economic interests.

Regrettably, because most state legislatures, like Congress, are controlled by the political party with a majority of representatives, many state legislatures practice gerrymandering for state and Congressional representatives.

I don't believe that group-based districting advances communities, nor does it enhance representative governance. But gerrymandering is a real problem, and needs to be addressed. The U.S. Constitution mandates districts for Senators. It may be time to also mandate how districts are to be set for Representatives.

APPENDIX B:
THE CONSTITUTION OF THE UNITED STATES

The United States Constitution
(Amended revisions included with strike-out text)

We the People of the United States, in Order to form a more perfect Union, establish Justice, insure domestic Tranquility, provide for the common defence, promote the general Welfare, and secure the Blessings of Liberty to ourselves and our Posterity, do ordain and establish this Constitution for the United States of America.

Article I
Section 1
All legislative Powers herein granted shall be vested in a Congress of the United States, which shall consist of a Senate and House of Representatives.

Section 2
1: The House of Representatives shall be composed of Members chosen every second Year by the People of the several States, and the Electors in each State shall have the Qualifications requisite for Electors of the most numerous Branch of the State Legislature.
2: No Person shall be a Representative who shall not have attained to the Age of twenty five Years, and been seven Years a Citizen of the United States, and who shall not, when elected, be an Inhabitant of that State in which he shall be chosen.
3: ~~Representatives and direct Taxes shall be apportioned among the several States which may be included within this Union, according to their respective Numbers, which shall be determined by adding to the whole Number of free Persons, including those bound to Service for a Term of Years, and excluding Indians not taxed, three fifths of~~

all other Persons. The actual Enumeration shall be made within three Years after the first Meeting of the Congress of the United States, and within every subsequent Term of ten Years, in such Manner as they shall by Law direct. The Number of Representatives shall not exceed one for every thirty Thousand, but each State shall have at Least one Representative; and until such enumeration shall be made, the State of New Hampshire shall be entitled to chuse three, Massachusetts eight, Rhode-Island and Providence Plantations one, Connecticut five, New-York six, New Jersey four, Pennsylvania eight, Delaware one, Maryland six, Virginia ten, North Carolina five, South Carolina five, and Georgia three.

4: When vacancies happen in the Representation from any State, the Executive Authority thereof shall issue Writs of Election to fill such Vacancies.

5: The House of Representatives shall chuse their Speaker and other Officers; and shall have the sole Power of Impeachment

.

Section 3

1: The Senate of the United States shall be composed of two Senators from each State, chosen by the Legislature thereof, for six Years; and each Senator shall have one Vote.

2: Immediately after they shall be assembled in Consequence of the first Election, they shall be divided as equally as may be into three Classes. The Seats of the Senators of the first Class shall be vacated at the Expiration of the second Year, of the second Class at the Expiration of the fourth Year, and of the third Class at the Expiration of the sixth Year, so that one third may be chosen every second Year; and if Vacancies happen by Resignation, or otherwise, during the Recess of the Legislature of any State, the Executive thereof may make temporary Appointments until the next Meeting of the Legislature, which shall then fill such Vacancies.

3: No Person shall be a Senator who shall not have attained to the Age of thirty Years, and been nine Years a Citizen of the United States, and who shall not, when elected, be an Inhabitant of that State for which he shall be chosen.

4: The Vice President of the United States shall be President of the Senate, but shall have no Vote, unless they be equally divided.

5: The Senate shall chuse their other Officers, and also a President pro tempore, in the Absence of the Vice President, or when he shall exercise the Office of President of the United States.

6: The Senate shall have the sole Power to try all Impeachments. When sitting for that Purpose, they shall be on Oath or Affirmation. When the President of the United States is tried, the Chief Justice shall preside: And no Person shall be convicted without the Concurrence of two thirds of the Members present.

7: Judgment in Cases of impeachment shall not extend further than to removal from Office, and disqualification to hold and enjoy any Office of honor, Trust or Profit under the United States: but the Party convicted shall nevertheless be liable and subject to Indictment, Trial, Judgment and Punishment, according to Law.

Section 4

1: The Times, Places and Manner of holding Elections for Senators and Representatives, shall be prescribed in each State by the Legislature thereof; but the Congress may at any time by Law make or alter such Regulations, except as to the Places of chusing Senators.

2: The Congress shall assemble at least once in every Year, ~~and such Meeting shall be on the first Monday in December~~, unless they shall by Law appoint a different Day.

Section 5

1: Each House shall be the Judge of the Elections, Returns and Qualifications of its own Members, and a Majority of each shall constitute a Quorum to do Business; but a smaller Number may adjourn from day to day, and may be authorized to compel the Attendance of absent Members, in such Manner, and under such Penalties as each House may provide.

2: Each House may determine the Rules of its Proceedings, punish its Members for disorderly Behaviour, and, with the Concurrence of two thirds, expel a Member.

3: Each House shall keep a Journal of its Proceedings, and from time to time publish the same, excepting such Parts as may in their Judgment require Secrecy; and the Yeas and Nays of the Members of either House on any question shall, at the Desire of one fifth of those Present, be entered on the Journal.

4: Neither House, during the Session of Congress, shall, without the Consent of the other, adjourn for more than three days, nor to any other Place than that in which the two Houses shall be sitting.

Section 6

1: The Senators and Representatives shall receive a Compensation for their Services, to be ascertained by Law, and paid out of the Treasury of the United States. They shall in all Cases, except Treason, Felony and Breach of the Peace, be privileged from Arrest during their Attendance at the Session of their respective Houses, and in going to and returning from the same; and for any Speech or Debate in either House, they shall not be questioned in any other Place.

2: No Senator or Representative shall, during the Time for which he was elected, be appointed to any civil Office under the Authority of the United States, which shall have been created, or the Emoluments whereof shall have been encreased during such time; and no Person holding any Office under the United States, shall be a Member of either House during his Continuance in Office.

Section 7

1: All Bills for raising Revenue shall originate in the House of Representatives; but the Senate may propose or concur with Amendments as on other Bills.

2: Every Bill which shall have passed the House of Representatives and the Senate, shall, before it become a Law, be presented to the President of the United States; If he approve he shall sign it, but if not he shall return it, with his Objections to that House in which it shall have originated, who shall enter the Objections at large on their Journal, and proceed to reconsider it. If after such Reconsideration two thirds of that House shall agree to pass the Bill, it shall be sent, together with the Objections, to the other House, by which it shall likewise be reconsidered, and if approved by two thirds of that House, it shall become a Law. But in all such Cases the Votes of both Houses shall be determined by yeas and Nays, and the Names of the Persons voting for and against the Bill shall be entered on the Journal of each House respectively. If any Bill shall not be returned by the President within ten Days (Sundays excepted) after it shall have been presented to him, the Same shall be a Law, in like Manner as if he had signed it, unless the Congress by their Adjournment prevent its Return, in which Case it shall not be a Law.

3: Every Order, Resolution, or Vote to which the Concurrence of the Senate and House of Representatives may be necessary (except on a question of Adjournment) shall be presented to the President of the United States; and before the Same shall take Effect, shall be approved by him, or being disapproved by him, shall be repassed by two thirds of the Senate and House of Representatives, according to the Rules and Limitations prescribed in the Case of a Bill.

Section 8

1: The Congress shall have Power To lay and collect Taxes, Duties, Imposts and Excises, to pay the Debts and provide for the common Defence and general Welfare of the United States; but all Duties, Imposts and Excises shall be uniform throughout the United States;

2: To borrow Money on the credit of the United States;

3: To regulate Commerce with foreign Nations, and among the several States, and with the Indian Tribes;

4: To establish an uniform Rule of Naturalization, and uniform Laws on the subject of Bankruptcies throughout the United States;

5: To coin Money, regulate the Value thereof, and of foreign Coin, and fix the Standard of Weights and Measures;

6: To provide for the Punishment of counterfeiting the Securities and current Coin of the United States;

7: To establish Post Offices and post Roads;

8: To promote the Progress of Science and useful Arts, by securing for limited Times to Authors and Inventors the exclusive Right to their respective Writings and Discoveries;

9: To constitute Tribunals inferior to the supreme Court;

10: To define and punish Piracies and Felonies committed on the high Seas, and Offences against the Law of Nations;

11: To declare War, grant Letters of Marque and Reprisal, and make Rules concerning Captures on Land and Water;

12: To raise and support Armies, but no Appropriation of Money to that Use shall be for a longer Term than two Years;

13: To provide and maintain a Navy;

14: To make Rules for the Government and Regulation of the land and naval Forces;

15: To provide for calling forth the Militia to execute the Laws of the Union, suppress Insurrections and repel Invasions;

16: To provide for organizing, arming, and disciplining, the Militia, and for governing such Part of them as may be employed in the Service of the United States, reserving to the States respectively, the Appointment of the Officers, and the Authority of training the Militia according to the discipline prescribed by Congress;

17: To exercise exclusive Legislation in all Cases whatsoever, over such District (not exceeding ten Miles square) as may, by Cession of particular States, and the Acceptance of Congress, become the Seat of the Government of the United States, and to exercise like Authority over all Places purchased by the Consent of the Legislature of the State in which the Same shall be, for the Erection of Forts, Magazines, Arsenals, dock-Yards, and other needful Buildings;--And

18: To make all Laws which shall be necessary and proper for carrying into Execution the foregoing Powers, and all other Powers vested by this Constitution in the Government of the United States, or in any Department or Officer thereof.

Section 9

1: ~~The Migration or Importation of such Persons as any of the States now existing shall think proper to admit, shall not be prohibited by the Congress prior to the Year one thousand eight hundred and eight, but a Tax or duty may be imposed on such Importation, not exceeding ten dollars for each Person.~~

2: The Privilege of the Writ of Habeas Corpus shall not be suspended, unless when in Cases of Rebellion or Invasion the public Safety may require it.

3: No Bill of Attainder or ex post facto Law shall be passed.

4: No Capitation, or other direct, Tax shall be laid, ~~unless in Proportion to the Census or Enumeration herein before directed to be taken.~~

5: No Tax or Duty shall be laid on Articles exported from any State.

6: No Preference shall be given by any Regulation of Commerce or Revenue to the Ports of one State over those of another: nor shall Vessels bound to, or from, one State, be obliged to enter, clear, or pay Duties in another.

7: No Money shall be drawn from the Treasury, but in Consequence of Appropriations made by Law; and a regular Statement and Account of the Receipts and Expenditures of all public Money shall be published from time to time.

8: No Title of Nobility shall be granted by the United States: And no Person holding any Office of Profit or Trust under them, shall, without the Consent of the Congress, accept of any present, Emolument, Office, or Title, of any kind whatever, from any King, Prince, or foreign State.

Section 10

1: No State shall enter into any Treaty, Alliance, or Confederation; grant Letters of Marque and Reprisal; coin Money; emit Bills of Credit; make any Thing but gold and silver Coin a Tender in Payment of Debts; pass any Bill of Attainder, ex post facto Law, or Law impairing the Obligation of Contracts, or grant any Title of Nobility.

2: No State shall, without the Consent of the Congress, lay any Imposts or Duties on Imports or Exports, except what may be absolutely necessary for executing it's inspection Laws: and the net Produce of all Duties and Imposts, laid by any State on Imports or Exports, shall be for the Use of the Treasury of the United States; and all such Laws shall be subject to the Revision and Controul of the Congress.

3: No State shall, without the Consent of Congress, lay any Duty of Tonnage, keep Troops, or Ships of War in time of Peace, enter into any Agreement or Compact with another State, or with a foreign Power, or engage in War, unless actually invaded, or in such imminent Danger as will not admit of delay.

Article II

Section 1

1: The executive Power shall be vested in a President of the United

States of America. He shall hold his Office during the Term of four Years, and, together with the Vice President, chosen for the same Term, be elected, as follows

2: Each State shall appoint, in such Manner as the Legislature thereof may direct, a Number of Electors, equal to the whole Number of Senators and Representatives to which the State may be entitled in the Congress: but no Senator or Representative, or Person holding an Office of Trust or Profit under the United States, shall be appointed an Elector.

3: ~~The Electors shall meet in their respective States, and vote by Ballot for two Persons, of whom one at least shall not be an Inhabitant of the same State with themselves. And they shall make a List of all the Persons voted for, and of the Number of Votes for each; which List they shall sign and certify, and transmit sealed to the Seat of the Government of the United States, directed to the President of the Senate. The President of the Senate shall, in the Presence of the Senate and House of Representatives, open all the Certificates, and the Votes shall then be counted. The Person having the greatest Number of Votes shall be the President, if such Number be a Majority of the whole Number of Electors appointed; and if there be more than one who have such Majority, and have an equal Number of Votes, then the House of Representatives shall immediately chuse by Ballot one of them for President; and if no Person have a Majority, then from the five highest on the List the said House shall in like Manner chuse the President. But in chusing the President, the Votes shall be taken by States, the Representation from each State having one Vote; A quorum for this Purpose shall consist of a Member or Members from two thirds of the States, and a Majority of all the States shall be necessary to a Choice. In every Case, after the Choice of the President, the Person having the greatest Number of Votes of the Electors shall be the Vice President. But if there should remain two or more who have equal Votes, the Senate shall chuse from them by Ballot the Vice President.~~

4: The Congress may determine the Time of chusing the Electors, and the Day on which they shall give their Votes; which Day shall be the same throughout the United States.

5: No Person except a natural born Citizen, or a Citizen of the United States, at the time of the Adoption of this Constitution, shall be eligible to the Office of President; neither shall any Person be eligible to that Office who shall not have attained to the Age of thirty five Years, and been fourteen Years a Resident within the United States.

6: ~~In Case of the Removal of the President from Office, or of his Death, Resignation, or Inability to discharge the Powers and Duties of the said Office,~~ the Same shall devolve on the VicePresident, and the Congress may by Law provide for the Case of Removal, Death, Resignation or Inability, both of the President and Vice President, declaring what Officer shall then act as President, and such Officer shall act accordingly, until the Disability be removed, or a President shall be elected.

7: The President shall, at stated Times, receive for his Services, a Compensation, which shall neither be encreased nor diminished during the Period for which he shall have been elected, and he shall not receive within that Period any other Emolument from the United States, or any of them.

8: Before he enter on the Execution of his Office, he shall take the following Oath or Affirmation:--"I do solemnly swear (or affirm) that I will faithfully execute the Office of President of the United States, and will to the best of my Ability, preserve, protect and defend the Constitution of the United States."

Section 2

1: The President shall be Commander in Chief of the Army and Navy of the United States, and of the Militia of the several States, when called into the actual Service of the United States; he may require the Opinion, in writing, of the principal Officer in each of the executive Departments, upon any Subject relating to the Duties of their respective Offices, and he shall have Power to grant Reprieves and Pardons for Offences against the United States, except in Cases of Impeachment.

2: He shall have Power, by and with the Advice and Consent of the Senate, to make Treaties, provided two thirds of the Senators present concur; and he shall nominate, and by and with the Advice and Consent of the Senate, shall appoint Ambassadors, other public Ministers and Consuls, Judges of the supreme Court, and all other

Officers of the United States, whose Appointments are not herein
otherwise provided for, and which shall be established by Law: but
the Congress may by Law vest the Appointment of such inferior Officers, as they think proper, in the President alone, in the Courts of
Law, or in the Heads of Departments.

3: The President shall have Power to fill up all Vacancies that may
happen during the Recess of the Senate, by granting Commissions
which shall expire at the End of their next Session.

Section 3

He shall from time to time give to the Congress Information of the
State of the Union, and recommend to their Consideration such
Measures as he shall judge necessary and expedient; he may, on ex-
traordinary Occasions, convene both Houses, or either of them, and
in Case of Disagreement between them, with Respect to the Time of
Adjournment, he may adjourn them to such Time as he shall think
proper; he shall receive Ambassadors and other public Ministers; he
shall take Care that the Laws be faithfully executed, and shall Commission all the Officers of the United States.

Section 4

The President, Vice President and all civil Officers of the United
States, shall be removed from Office on Impeachment for, and Conviction of, Treason, Bribery, or other high Crimes and Misdemean-
ors.

Article III

Section 1

The judicial Power of the United States, shall be vested in one supreme Court, and in such inferior Courts as the Congress may from
time to time ordain and establish. The Judges, both of the supreme
and inferior Courts, shall hold their Offices during good Behaviour,
and shall, at stated Times, receive for their Services, a Compensation, which shall not be diminished during their Continuance in Office.

Section 2

1: The judicial Power shall extend to all Cases, in Law and Equity, arising under this Constitution, the Laws of the United States, and Treaties made, or which shall be made, under their Authority;--to all Cases affecting Ambassadors, other public Ministers and Consuls;--to all Cases of admiralty and maritime Jurisdiction;--to Controversies to which the United States shall be a Party;--to Controversies between two or more States;--~~between a State and Citizens of another State~~; --between Citizens of different States, --between Citizens of the same State claiming Lands under Grants of different States, and between a State, or the Citizens thereof, and foreign States, Citizens or Subjects.

2: In all Cases affecting Ambassadors, other public Ministers and Consuls, and those in which a State shall be Party, the supreme Court shall have original Jurisdiction. In all the other Cases before mentioned, the supreme Court shall have appellate Jurisdiction, both as to Law and Fact, with such Exceptions, and under such Regulations as the Congress shall make.

3: The Trial of all Crimes, except in Cases of Impeachment, shall be by Jury; and such Trial shall be held in the State where the said Crimes shall have been committed; but when not committed within any State, the Trial shall be at such Place or Places as the Congress may by Law have directed.

Section 3

1: Treason against the United States, shall consist only in levying War against them, or in adhering to their Enemies, giving them Aid and Comfort. No Person shall be convicted of Treason unless on the Testimony of two Witnesses to the same overt Act, or on Confession in open Court.

2: The Congress shall have Power to declare the Punishment of Treason, but no Attainder of Treason shall work Corruption of Blood, or Forfeiture except during the Life of the Person attainted.

Article IV

Section 1

Full Faith and Credit shall be given in each State to the public Acts, Records, and judicial Proceedings of every other State. And the Congress may by general Laws prescribe the Manner in which such Acts, Records and Proceedings shall be proved, and the Effect thereof.

Section 2

1: The Citizens of each State shall be entitled to all Privileges and Immunities of Citizens in the several States.

2: A Person charged in any State with Treason, Felony, or other Crime, who shall flee from Justice, and be found in another State, shall on Demand of the executive Authority of the State from which he fled, be delivered up, to be removed to the State having Jurisdiction of the Crime.

3: ~~No Person held to Service or Labour in one State, under the Laws thereof, escaping into another, shall, in Consequence of any Law or Regulation therein, be discharged from such Service or Labour, but shall be delivered up on Claim of the Party to whom such Service or Labour may be due~~.

Section 3

1: New States may be admitted by the Congress into this Union; but no new State shall be formed or erected within the Jurisdiction of any other State; nor any State be formed by the Junction of two or more States, or Parts of States, without the Consent of the Legislatures of the States concerned as well as of the Congress.

2: The Congress shall have Power to dispose of and make all needful Rules and Regulations respecting the Territory or other Property belonging to the United States; and nothing in this Constitution shall be so construed as to Prejudice any Claims of the United States, or of any particular State.

Section 4

The United States shall guarantee to every State in this Union a Republican Form of Government, and shall protect each of them against Invasion; and on Application of the Legislature, or of the Executive (when the Legislature cannot be convened) against domestic Violence.

Article V

The Congress, whenever two thirds of both Houses shall deem it necessary, shall propose Amendments to this Constitution, or, on the Application of the Legislatures of two thirds of the several States, shall call a Convention for proposing Amendments, which, in either Case, shall be valid to all Intents and Purposes, as Part of this Constitution, when ratified by the Legislatures of three fourths of the several States, or by Conventions in three fourths thereof, as the one or the other Mode of Ratification may be proposed by the Congress; Provided that no Amendment which may be made prior to the Year One thousand eight hundred and eight shall in any Manner affect the first and fourth Clauses in the Ninth Section of the first Article; and that no State, without its Consent, shall be deprived of its equal Suffrage in the Senate.

Article VI

1: All Debts contracted and Engagements entered into, before the Adoption of this Constitution, shall be as valid against the United States under this Constitution, as under the Confederation.
2: This Constitution, and the Laws of the United States which shall be made in Pursuance thereof; and all Treaties made, or which shall be made, under the Authority of the United States, shall be the supreme Law of the Land; and the Judges in every State shall be bound thereby, any Thing in the Constitution or Laws of any State to the Contrary notwithstanding.
3: The Senators and Representatives before mentioned, and the Members of the several State Legislatures, and all executive and judicial Officers, both of the United States and of the several States, shall be bound by Oath or Affirmation, to support this Constitution; but no religious Test shall ever be required as a Qualification to any Office or public Trust under the United States.

Article VII

The Ratification of the Conventions of nine States, shall be suffi-cient for the Establishment of this Constitution between the States so ratifying the Same.

Amendments

Amendment I
Congress shall make no law respecting an establishment of religion, or prohibiting the free exercise thereof; or abridging the freedom of speech, or of the press; or the right of the people peaceably to as-semble, and to petition the Government for a redress of grievances.

Amendment II
A well regulated Militia, being necessary to the security of a free State, the right of the people to keep and bear Arms, shall not be infringed.

Amendment III
No Soldier shall, in time of peace be quartered in any house, without the consent of the Owner, nor in time of war, but in a manner to be prescribed by law.

Amendment IV
The right of the people to be secure in their persons, houses, papers, and effects, against unreasonable searches and seizures, shall not be violated, and no Warrants shall issue, but upon probable cause, sup-ported by Oath or affirmation, and particularly describing the place to be searched, and the persons or things to be seized.

Amendment V
No person shall be held to answer for a capital, or otherwise infa-mous crime, unless on a presentment or indictment of a Grand Jury, except in cases arising in the land or naval forces, or in the Militia, when in actual service in time of War or public danger; nor shall any person be subject for the same offence to be twice put in jeopardy

of life or limb; nor shall be compelled in any criminal case to be a witness against himself, nor be deprived of life, liberty, or property, without due process of law; nor shall private property be taken for public use, without just compensation.

Amendment VI
In all criminal prosecutions, the accused shall enjoy the right to a speedy and public trial, by an impartial jury of the State and district wherein the crime shall have been committed, which district shall have been previously ascertained by law, and to be informed of the nature and cause of the accusation; to be confronted with the witnesses against him; to have compulsory process for obtaining witnesses in his favor, and to have the Assistance of Counsel for his defence.

Amendment VII
In Suits at common law, where the value in controversy shall exceed twenty dollars, the right of trial by jury shall be preserved, and no fact tried by a jury, shall be otherwise re-examined in any Court of the United States, than according to the rules of the common law.

Amendment VIII
Excessive bail shall not be required, nor excessive fines imposed, nor cruel and unusual punishments inflicted.

Amendment IX
The enumeration in the Constitution, of certain rights, shall not be construed to deny or disparage others retained by the people.

Amendment X
The powers not delegated to the United States by the Constitution, nor prohibited by it to the States, are reserved to the States respectively, or to the people
.

Amendment XI
The Judicial power of the United States shall not be construed to extend to any suit in law or equity, commenced or prosecuted against

one of the United States by Citizens of another State, or by Citizens or Subjects of any Foreign State.

Amendment XII

The Electors shall meet in their respective states, and vote by ballot for President and Vice-President, one of whom, at least, shall not be an inhabitant of the same state with themselves; they shall name in their ballots the person voted for as President, and in distinct ballots the person voted for as Vice-President, and they shall make distinct lists of all persons voted for as President, and of all persons voted for as Vice-President, and of the number of votes for each, which lists they shall sign and certify, and transmit sealed to the seat of the government of the United States, directed to the President of the Senate;--The President of the Senate shall, in the presence of the Senate and House of Representatives, open all the certificates and the votes shall then be counted;--The person having the greatest number of votes for President, shall be the President, if such number be a majority of the whole number of Electors appointed; and if no person have such majority, then from the persons having the highest numbers not exceeding three on the list of those voted for as President, the House of Representatives shall choose immediately, by ballot, the President. But in choosing the President, the votes shall be taken by states, the representation from each state having one vote; a quorum for this purpose shall consist of a member or members from two-thirds of the states, and a majority of all the states shall be necessary to a choice. ~~And if the House of Representatives shall not choose a President whenever the right of choice shall devolve upon them, before the fourth day of March next following, then the Vice-President shall act as President, as in the case of the death or other constitutional disability of the President~~. --The person having the greatest number of votes as Vice-President, shall be the Vice-President, if such number be a majority of the whole number of Electors appointed, and if no person have a majority, then from the two highest numbers on the list, the Senate shall choose the Vice-President; a quorum for the purpose shall consist of two-thirds of the whole number of Senators, and a majority of the whole number shall be necessary to a choice. But no person constitutionally ineligible to the office of President shall be eligible to that of Vice-President of the United States.

Amendment XIII
Neither slavery nor involuntary servitude, except as a punishment for crime whereof the party shall have been duly convicted, shall exist within the United States, or any place subject to their jurisdiction. Congress shall have power to enforce this article by appropriate legislation.

Amendment XIV
1: All persons born or naturalized in the United States, and subject to the jurisdiction thereof, are citizens of the United States and of the State wherein they reside. No State shall make or enforce any law which shall abridge the privileges or immunities of citizens of the United States; nor shall any State deprive any person of life, liberty, or property, without due process of law; nor deny to any person within its jurisdiction the equal protection of the laws.
2: Representatives shall be apportioned among the several States according to their respective numbers, counting the whole number of persons in each State, excluding Indians not taxed. But when the right to vote at any election for the choice of electors for President and Vice President of the United States, Representatives in Congress, the Executive and Judicial officers of a State, or the members of the Legislature thereof, is denied to any of the ~~male~~ inhabitants of such State, being ~~twenty-one~~ years of age, and citizens of the United States, or in any way abridged, except for participation in rebellion, or other crime, the basis of representation therein shall be reduced in the proportion which the number of such ~~male~~ citizens shall bear to the whole number of ~~male~~ citizens ~~twenty-one~~ years of age in such State.
3: No person shall be a Senator or Representative in Congress, or elector of President and Vice President, or hold any office, civil or military, under the United States, or under any State, who, having previously taken an oath, as a member of Congress, or as an officer of the United States, or as a member of any State legislature, or as an executive or judicial officer of any State, to support the Constitution

of the United States, shall have engaged in insurrection or rebellion against the same, or given aid or comfort to the enemies thereof. But Congress may by a vote of two-thirds of each House, remove such disability.

4: The validity of the public debt of the United States, authorized by law, including debts incurred for payment of pensions and bounties for services in suppressing insurrection or rebellion, shall not be questioned. But neither the United States nor any State shall assume or pay any debt or obligation incurred in aid of insurrection or rebellion against the United States, or any claim for the loss or emancipation of any slave; but all such debts, obligations and claims shall be held illegal and void.

5: The Congress shall have power to enforce, by appropriate legislation, the provisions of this article.

Amendment XV
The right of citizens of the United States to vote shall not be denied or abridged by the United States or by any State on account of race, color, or previous condition of servitude.

The Congress shall have power to enforce this article by appropriate legislation.

Amendment XVI
The Congress shall have power to lay and collect taxes on incomes, from whatever source derived, without apportionment among the several States, and without regard to any census or enumeration.

Amendment XVII
1: The Senate of the United States shall be composed of two Senators from each State, elected by the people thereof, for six years; and each Senator shall have one vote. The electors in each State shall have the qualifications requisite for electors of the most numerous branch of the State legislatures.

2: When vacancies happen in the representation of any State in the Senate, the executive authority of such State shall issue writs of election to fill such vacancies: Provided, That the legislature of any State may empower the executive thereof to make temporary appointments until the people fill the vacancies by election as the legislature may direct.

3: This Amendment shall not be so construed as to affect the election or term of any Senator chosen before it becomes valid as part of the Constitution.

Amendment XVIII
1: After one year from the ratification of this article the manufacture, sale, or transportation of intoxicating liquors within, the importation thereof into, or the exportation thereof from the United States and all territory subject to the jurisdiction thereof for beverage purposes is hereby prohibited.
2: The Congress and the several States shall have concurrent power to enforce this article by appropriate legislation.
3: This article shall be inoperative unless it shall have been ratified as an Amendment to the Constitution by the legislatures of the several States, as provided in the Constitution, within seven years from the date of the submission hereof to the States by the Congress.

Amendment XIX
The right of citizens of the United States to vote shall not be denied or abridged by the United States or by any State on account of sex. Congress shall have power to enforce this article by appropriate legislation.

Amendment XX
1: The terms of the President and Vice President shall end at noon on the 20th day of January, and the terms of Senators and Representatives at noon on the 3d day of January, of the years in which such terms would have ended if this article had not been ratified; and the terms of their successors shall then begin.
2: The Congress shall assemble at least once in every year, and such meeting shall begin at noon on the 3d day of January, unless they shall by law appoint a different day.
3: If, at the time fixed for the beginning of the term of the President, the President elect shall have died, the Vice President elect shall become President. If a President shall not have been chosen before

the time fixed for the beginning of his term, or if the President elect shall have failed to qualify, then the Vice President elect shall act as President until a President shall have qualified; and the Congress may by law provide for the case wherein neither a President elect nor a Vice President elect shall have qualified, declaring who shall then act as President, or the manner in which one who is to act shall be selected, and such person shall act accordingly until a President or Vice President shall have qualified.

4: The Congress may by law provide for the case of the death of any of the persons from whom the House of Representatives may choose a President whenever the right of choice shall have devolved upon them, and for the case of the death of any of the persons from whom the Senate may choose a Vice President whenever the right of choice shall have devolved upon them.

5: Sections 1 and 2 shall take effect on the 15th day of October following the ratification of this article.

6: This article shall be inoperative unless it shall have been ratified as an Amendment to the Constitution by the legislatures of three-fourths of the several States within seven years from the date of its submission.

Amendment XXI

1: The eighteenth article of Amendment to the Constitution of the United States is hereby repealed.

2: The transportation or importation into any State, Territory, or possession of the United States for delivery or use therein of intoxicating liquors, in violation of the laws thereof, is hereby prohibited.

3: This article shall be inoperative unless it shall have been ratified as an Amendment to the Constitution by conventions in the several States, as provided in the Constitution, within seven years from the date of the submission hereof to the States by the Congress.

Amendment XXII

1: No person shall be elected to the office of the President more than twice, and no person who has held the office of President, or acted as President, for more than two years of a term to which some other person was elected President shall be elected to the office of the President more than once. But this article shall not apply to any person holding the office of President when this article was proposed by the Congress, and shall not prevent any person who may be holding the office of President, or acting as President, during the term within which this article becomes operative from holding the office of President or acting as President during the remainder of such term.

2: This article shall be inoperative unless it shall have been ratified as an Amendment to the Constitution by the legislatures of three-fourths of the several states within seven years from the date of its submission to the states by the Congress.

Amendment XXIII

1: The District constituting the seat of government of the United States shall appoint in such manner as the Congress may direct: A number of electors of President and Vice President equal to the whole number of Senators and Representatives in Congress to which the District would be entitled if it were a state, but in no event more than the least populous state; they shall be in addition to those appointed by the states, but they shall be considered, for the purposes of the election of President and Vice President, to be electors appointed by a state; and they shall meet in the District and perform such duties as provided by the twelfth article of Amendment.

2: The Congress shall have power to enforce this article by appropriate legislation.

Amendment XXIV

1. The right of citizens of the United States to vote in any primary or other election for President or Vice President, for electors for President or Vice President, or for Senator or Representative in Congress, shall not be denied or abridged by the United States or any state by reason of failure to pay any poll tax or other tax.

2. The Congress shall have power to enforce this article by appropriate legislation.

Amendment XXV

1: In case of the removal of the President from office or of his death or resignation, the Vice President shall become President.

2: Whenever there is a vacancy in the office of the Vice President, the President shall nominate a Vice President who shall take office upon confirmation by a majority vote of both Houses of Congress.

3: Whenever the President transmits to the President pro tempore of the Senate and the Speaker of the House of Representatives his written declaration that he is unable to discharge the powers and duties of his office, and until he transmits to them a written declaration to the contrary, such powers and duties shall be discharged by the Vice President as Acting President.

4: Whenever the Vice President and a majority of either the principal officers of the executive departments or of such other body as Congress may by law provide, transmit to the President pro tempore of the Senate and the Speaker of the House of Representatives their written declaration that the President is unable to discharge the powers and duties of his office, the Vice President shall immediately assume the powers and duties of the office as Acting President.

Thereafter, when the President transmits to the President pro tempore of the Senate and the Speaker of the House of Representatives his written declaration that no inability exists, he shall resume the powers and duties of his office unless the Vice President and a majority of either the principal officers of the executive department or of such other body as Congress may by law provide, transmit within four days to the President pro tempore of the Senate and the Speaker of the House of Representatives their written declaration that the President is unable to discharge the powers and duties of his office. Thereupon Congress shall decide the issue, assembling within forty-eight hours for that purpose if not in session. If the Congress, within twenty-one days after receipt of the latter written declaration, or, if Congress is not in session, within twenty-one days after Congress is required to assemble, determines by two-thirds vote of both Houses that the President is unable to discharge the powers and duties of his office, the Vice President shall continue to discharge the same as Acting President; otherwise, the President shall resume the powers and duties of his office.

Amendment XXVI

1: The right of citizens of the United States, who are 18 years of age or older, to vote, shall not be denied or abridged by the United States or any state on account of age.

2: The Congress shall have the power to enforce this article by appropriate legislation.

Amendment XXVII

No law varying the compensation for the services of the Senators and Representatives shall take effect until an election of Representatives shall have intervened.

APPENDIX C:
STATE RESOLUTIONS RATIFY-
ING THE FIRST CONSTITUTION

STATE RESOLUTIONS RATIFYING THE CONSTITUTION

All of the original thirteen states wrote and approved resolutions which ratified the original Constitution. Five of the state resolutions were bare-bones documents focused only on documenting ratification of the Constitution. Seven state resolutions included interpretations of the Constitution's new framework, or proposed specific Amendments to be added to the Constitution, or both.

The delegates who attended the original Constitutional Convention generally agreed that the Constitution should include what we now call the Bill of Rights. But the major demand of the time, and the major concern of the new Constitution, was to replace the unworkable Articles of Confederation with a truly workable Federal Government, while also ensuring the new Federal Government would remain respectful of State Governments, and mindful of citizens' rights and freedoms. Most delegates believed that working out structural governmental details of the Constitution was enough of a challenge without also refining a statement of rights. So they agreed that the first Congress should propose a number of Amendments which would comprise a Bill of Rights. To move this process forward, seven states suggested specific language for these Amendments in their resolutions of ratification.

The Bill of Rights as finally written and ratified incorporated many of the recommendations from the States. But many of the State recommendations never found a home in either the final Bill of Rights, or in later Amendments. At the time, many legislators thought some of the suggested additions were unnecessary, because they believed that the meaning of the Constitution was well understood, and further clarification with additional words was unnecessary. There were probably other State recommendations that simply wouldn't gather sufficient popular support.

Most students of the Constitution are familiar with the Federalist Papers as a thorough commentary on the Constitution, and the intent of its words. These State resolutions provide additional insights. For this reason, the ratification resolutions of seven of the thirteen original states are reprinted in this appendix. The text was copied from the Yale Law School Avalon Project web site, where they were reprinted from Documentary History of the Constitution (1894). They are in alphabetical order by State name: Massachusetts, North Carolina, New Hampshire, New York, Rhode Island, South Carolina and Virginia.

Ratification of the Constitution by the
State of Massachusetts; February 6, 1788

In Convention of the delegates of the People of the Commonwealth of Massachusetts February 6th 1788.

The Convention have impartially discussed, & fully considered the Constitution for the United States of America, reported to Congress by the Convention of Delegates from the United States of America, & submitted to us by a resolution of the General Court of the said Commonwealth, passed the twenty fifth day of October last past, & acknowledging with grateful hearts, the goodness of the Supreme Ruler of the Universe in affording the People of the United States in the course of his providence an opportunity deliberately & peaceably without fraud or surprize of entering into an explicit & solemn Compact with each other by assenting to & ratifying a New Constitution in order to form a more perfect Union, establish Justice, insure Domestic tranquillity, provide for the common defence, promote the general welfare & secure the blessings of Liberty to themselves & their posterity; Do in the name & in behalf of the People of the Commonwealth of Massachusetts assent to & ratify the said Constitution for the United States of America.

And as it is the opinion of this Convention that certain Amendments & alterations in the said Constitution would remove the fears & quiet the apprehensions of many of the good people of this Commonwealth & more effectually guard against an undue administration of the Federal Government, The Convention do therefore recommend that the following alterations & provisions be introduced into the said Constitution.

First, That it be explicitly declared that all Powers not expressly delegated by the aforesaid Constitution are reserved to the several States to be by them exercised.

Secondly, That there shall be one representative to every thirty thousand persons according to the Census mentioned in the Constitution until the whole number of the Representatives amounts to Two hundred.

Thirdly, That Congress do not exercise the powers vested in them by the fourth Section of the first article, but in cases when a State shall neglect or refuse to make the regulations therein mentioned or shall make regulations subversive of the rights of the People to a free & equal representation in Congress agreeably to the Constitution.

Fourthly, That Congress do not lay direct Taxes but when the Monies arising from the Impost & Excise are insufficient for the publick exigencies nor then until Congress shall have first made a requisition upon the States to assess levy & pay their respective proportions of such Requisition agreeably to the Census fixed in the said Constitution; in such way & manner as the Legislature of the States shall think best, & in such case if any State shall neglect or refuse to pay its proportion pursuant to such requisition then Congress may assess & levy such State's proportion together with interest thereon at the rate of Six per cent per annum from the time of payment prescribed in such requisition

Fifthly, That Congress erect no Company of Merchants with exclusive advantages of commerce.

Sixthly, That no person shall be tried for any Crime by which he may incur an infamous punishment or loss of life until he be first indicted by a Grand Jury, except in such cases as may arise in the Government & regulation of the Land & Naval forces.

Seventhly, The Supreme Judicial Federal Court shall have no jurisdiction of Causes between Citizens of different States unless the matter in dispute whether it concerns the realty or personally be of the value of three thousand dollars at the least. nor shall the Federal Judicial Powers extend to any actions between Citizens of different States where the matter in dispute whether it concerns the Realty or personally is not of the value of Fifteen hundred dollars at the least.

Eighthly, In civil actions between Citizens of different States every issue of fact arising in Actions at common law shall be tried by a Jury if the parties or either of them request it.

Ninthly, Congress shall at no time consent that any person holding an office of trust or profit under the United States shall accept of a title of Nobility or any other title or office from any King, prince or Foreign State.

And the Convention do in the name & in behalf of the People of this Commonwealth enjoin it upon their Representatives in Congress at all times until the alterations & provisions aforesaid have been considered agreeably to the Fifth article of the said Constitution to exert all their influence & use all reasonable & legal methods to obtain a ratification of the said alterations & provisions in such manner as is provided in the said Article.

And that the United States in Congress Assembled may have due notice of the Assent & Ratification of the said Constitution by this Convention it is, Resolved, that the Assent & Ratification aforesaid be engrossed on Parchment together with the recommendation & injunction aforesaid & with this resolution & that His Excellency John Hancock Esqr President & the Hong William Cushing Esqr Vice President, of this Convention transmit the same, counter-signed by the Secretary of the Convention under their hands & seals to the United States in Congress Assembled

JOHN HANCOCK President
WM CUSHING Vice President
GEORGE RICHARDS MINOT, Secretary.

Pursuant to the Resolution aforesaid WE the President & Vice President abovenamed Do hereby transmit to the United States in Congress Assembled, the same Resolution with the above Assent and Ratification of the Constitution aforesaid for the United States, And the recommendation & injunction above specified.

In Witness whereof We have hereunto set our hands & Seals at Boston in the Commonwealth aforesaid this Seventh day of February Anno Domini, one thousand Seven Hundred & Eighty eight, and in the Twelfth year of the Independence of the United States of America.

JOHN HANCOCK President
Wm CUSHING Vice President

Ratification of the Constitution by the State of North Carolina; November 21, 1789

In Convention, August I, 1788.

Resolved, That a Declaration of Rights, asserting and securing from encroachment the great Principles of civil and religious Liberty, and the unalienable Rights of the People, together with Amendments to the most ambiguous and exceptional Parts of the said Constitution of Government, ought to be laid before Congress, and the Convention of the States that shall or may be called for the Purpose of Amending the said Constitution, for their consideration, previous to the Ratification of the Constitution aforesaid, on the part of the State of North Carolina.

DECLARATION OF RIGHTS

1st That there are certain natural rights of which men, when they form a social compact, cannot deprive or divest their posterity, among which are the enjoyment of life, and liberty, with the means of acquiring, possessing, and protecting property, and pursuing and obtaining happiness and safety.

2d. That all power is naturally vested in, and consequently derived from the people; that magistrates therefore are their trustees, and agents, and at all times amenable to them.

3d. That Government ought to be instituted for the common benefit, protection and security of the people; and that the doctrine of non-resistance against arbitrary power and oppression is absurd, slavish, and destructive to the good and happiness of mankind.

4th That no man or set of men are entitled to exclusive or separate public emoluments or privileges from the community, but in consideration of public services; which not being descendible, neither ought the offices of magistrate, legislator or judge, or any other public office to be hereditary.

5th. That the legislative, executive and judiciary powers of government should be separate and distinct, and that the members of the two first may be restrained from oppression by feeling and participating the public burthens, they should at fixed periods be reduced to a private station, return into the mass of the people; and the vacancies be supplied by certain and regular elections; in which all or any part of the former members to be eligible or ineligible, as the rules of the Constitution of Government, and the laws shall direct.

6th. That elections of Representatives in the legislature ought to be free and frequent, and all men having sufficient evidence of permanent common interest with, and attachment to the community, ought to have the right of suffrage: and no aid, charge, tax or fee can be set, rated, or levied upon the people without their own consent, or that of their representatives, so elected, nor can they be bound by any law, to which they have not in like manner assented for the public good.

7th. That all power of suspending laws, or the execution of laws by any authority without the consent of the representatives, of the people in the Legislature, is injurious to their rights, and ought not to be exercised.

8th. That in all capital and criminal prosecutions, a man hath a right to demand the cause and nature of his accusation, to be confronted with the accusers and witnesses, to call for evidence and be allowed counsel in his favor, and to a fair and speedy trial by an impartial jury of his vicinage, without whose unanimous consent he cannot be found guilty (except in the government of the land and naval forces) nor can he be compelled to give evidence against himself.

9th That no freeman ought to be taken, imprisoned, or disseized of his freehold, liberties, privileges or franchises, or outlawed or exiled, or in any manner destroyed or deprived of his life, liberty, or property but by the law of the land.

10th. That every freeman restrained of his liberty is entitled to a remedy to inquire into the lawfulness thereof, and to remove the same, if unlawful, and that such remedy ought not to be denied nor delayed.

11th. That in controversies respecting property, and in suits between man and man, the ancient trial by jury is one of the greatest securities to the rights of the people, and ought to remain sacred and inviolable.

12th. That every freeman ought to find a certain remedy by recourse to the laws for all injuries and wrongs he may receive in his person, property, or character. He ought to obtain right and justice freely without sale, completely and without denial, promptly and without delay, and that all establishments, or regulations contravening these rights, are oppressive and unjust.

13th. That excessive bail ought not to be required, nor excessive fines imposed, nor cruel and unusual punishments inflicted,

14th. That every freeman has a right to be secure from all unreasonable searches, and seizures of his person, his papers, and property: all warrants therefore to search suspected places, or seize any freeman, his papers or property, without information upon oath (or affirmation of a person religiously scrupulous of taking an oath) of legal and sufficient cause, are grievous and oppressive, and all general warrants to search suspected places, or to apprehend any suspected person without specially naming or describing the place or person, are dangerous and ought not to be granted.

15th. That the people have a right peaceably to assemble together to consult for the common good, or to instruct their representatives; and that every freeman has a right to petition or apply to the Legislature for redress of grievances.

16th. That the people have a right to freedom of speech, and of writing and publishing their sentiments; that the freedom of the press is one of the greatest bulwarks of Liberty, and ought not to be violated.

17th. That the people have a right to keep and bear arms; that a well regulated militia composed of the body of the people, trained to arms, is the proper, natural and safe defence of a free state. That standing armies in time of peace are dangerous to Liberty, and therefore ought to be avoided, as far as the circumstances and protection of the community will admit; and that in all cases, the military should be under strict subordination to, and governed by the civil power.

18th. That no soldier in time of peace ought to be quartered in any house without the consent of the owner, and in time of war in such manner only as the Laws direct

19th. That any person religiously scrupulous of bearing arms ought to be exempted upon payment of an equivalent to employ another to bear arms in his stead.

20th. That religion, or the duty which we owe to our Creator, and the manner of discharging it, can be directed only by reason and conviction, not by force or violence, and therefore all men have an equal, natural and unalienable right to the free exercise of religion according to the dictates of conscience, and that no particular religious sect or society ought to be favoured or established by law in preference to others.

Amendments TO THE CONSTITUTION

I. THAT each state in the union shall, respectively, retain every power, jurisdiction and right, which is not by this constitution delegated to the Congress of the United States, or to the departments of the Federal Government.

II. That there shall be one representative for every 30.000, according to the enumeration or census, mentioned in the constitution, until the whole number of representatives amounts to two hundred; after which, that number shall be continued or increased, as Congress shall direct, upon the principles fixed in the constitution, by apportioning the representatives of each state to some greater number of people from time to time, as population encreases.

III. When Congress shall lay direct taxes or excises, they shall immediately inform the executive power of each state, of the quota of such State, according to the census herein directed, which is proposed to be thereby raised: And if the legislature of any state shall pass a law, which shall be effectual for raismg such quota at the time required by Congress, the taxes and excises laid by Congress shall not be collected in such state.

IV. That the members of the senate and house of representatives shall be ineligible to, and incapable of holding any civil office under the authority of the United States, during the time for which they shall, respectively, be elected.

V. That the journals of the proceedings of the senate and house of representatives shall be published at least once in every year, except such parts thereof relating to treaties, alliances, or military operations, as in their judgment require secrecy.

VI. That a regular statement and account of the receipts and expenditures of the public money shall be published at least once in every year.

VII. That no commercial treaty shall be ratified without the concurrence of two-thirds of the whole number of the members of the Senate: And no treaty, ceding, contracting, or restraining or suspending the territorial rights or claims of the United States, or any of them or their, or any of their rights or claims to fishing in the American seas, or navigating the American rivers shall be made, but in cases of the most urgent and extreme necessity; nor shall any such treaty be ratified without the concurrence of three-fourths of the whole number of the members of both houses respectively.

VIII. That no navigation law, or law regulating commerce shall be passed without the consent of two-thirds of the members present in both houses.

IX. That no standing army or regular troops shall be raised or kept up in time of peace, without the consent of two thirds of the members present in both houses.

X. That no soldier shall be enlisted for any longer term than four years, except in time of war, and then for no longer term than the continuance of the war

XI. That each state, respectively, shall have the power to provide for organizing, arming and disciplining its own militia whensoever Congress shall omit or neglect to provide for the same. That the militia shall not be subject to martial law, except when in actual service in time of war, invasion or rebellion: And when not in the actual service of the United States, shall be subject only to such fines, penalties, and punishments as shall be directed or inflicted by the laws of its own state.

XII. That Congress shall not declare any state to be in rebellion without the consent of at least two-thirds of all the members present of both houses.

XIII. That the exclusive power of Legislation given to Congress over the federal town and its adjacent district, and other places, purchased or to be purchased by Congress, of any of the states, shall extend only to such regulations as respect the police and good government thereof.

XIV. That no person shall be capable of being president of the United States for more than eight years in any term of sixteen years.

XV. That the judicial power of the United States shall be vested in one supreme court, and in such courts of admiralty as Congress may from time to time ordain and establish in any of the different states. The judicial power shall extend to all cases in law and equity, arising under treaties made, or which shall be made under the authority of the United States; to all cases affecting ambassadors, other foreign ministers and consuls; to all cases of admiralty, and maritime jurisdiction; to controversies to which the United States shall be a party; to controversies between two or more stares, and between parties claiming lands under the grants of different states. In all cases affecting ambassadors, other foreign ministers and consuls, and those in which a state shall be a party; the supreme court shall have original jurisdiction, in all other cases before mentioned; the supreme court shall have appellate jurisdiction as to matters of law only, except in cases of equity, and of admiralty and maritime jurisdiction, in which the supreme court shall have appelate jurisdiction both as to law and fact, with such exceptions, and under such regulations as the Congress shall make. But the judicial power of the United States shall extend to no case where the cause of action shall have originated before the ratification of this constitution, except in disputes between states about their territory; disputes between persons claiming lands under the grants of different states, and suits for debts due to the united states.

XVI. That in criminal prosecutions, no man shall be restrained in the exercise of the usual and accustomed right of challenging or excepting to the jury.

XVII. That Congress shall not alter, modify, or interfere in the times, places, or manner of holding elections for senators and representatives, or either of them, except when the legislature of any state shall neglect, refuse or be disabled by invasion or rebellion, to prescribe the same.

XVIII. That those clauses which declare that Congress shall not exercise certain powers, be not interpreted in any manner whatsoever to extend the powers of Congress; but that they be construed either as making exceptions to the specified powers where this shall be the case, or otherwise, as inserted merely for greater caution.

XIX. That the laws ascertaining the compensation of senators and representatives for their services be posponed in their operation, until after the election of representatives immediately succeeding the passing thereof, that excepted, which shall first be passed on the subject,

XX. That some tribunal, other than the senate, be provided for trying impeachments of senators.

XXI That the salary of a judge shall not be increased or diminished during his continuance in once, otherwise than by general regulations of salary which may take place, on a revision of the subject at stated periods of not less than seven years, to commence from the time such salaries shall be first ascertained by Congress.

XXII. That Congress erect no company of merchants with exclusive advantages of commerce.

XXIII. That no treaties which shall be directly opposed to the existing laws of the United States in Congress assembled, shall be valid until such laws shall be repealed, or made conformable to such Meaty; nor shall any Meaty be valid which is contradictory to the constitution of the United States.

XXIV. That the latter part of the fifth paragraph of the 9th section of the first article be altered to read thus,-Nor shall vessels bound to a particular state be obliged to enter or pay duties in any other; nor when bound from any one of the States be obliged to clear in another.

XXV. That Congress shall not directly or indirectly, either by themselves or thro' the judiciary, interfere with any one of the states in the redemption of paper money already emitted and now in circulation, or in liquidating and discharging the public securities of any one of the states: But each and every state shall have the exclusive right of making such laws and regulations for the above purposes as they shall think proper.

XXVI That Congress shall not introduce foreign troops into the United States without the consent of two-thirds of the members present of both houses.

SAM JOHNSTON President,

By order

J HUNT Secretary . . .

IN CONVENTION Whereas The General Convention which met in Philadelphia in Pursuance of a recommendation of Congress, did recommend to the Citizens of the United States a Constitution or form of Government in the following words Vizt.

Resolved, that this Convention in behalf of the freemen, citizens and inhabitants of the State of North Carolina, do adopt and ratify the said Constitution and form of Government. Done in Convention this 21 day of November 1789.

SAM JOHNSTON, President of the Convention

J HUNT Secretaries

JAMES TAYLOR

Ratification of the Constitution by the State of New Hampshire; June 21, 1788

In Convention of the Delegates of the People of the State of New-Hampshire June the Twenty first 1788.

The Convention haveing Impartially discussed and fully considered the Constitution for the United States of America, reported to Congress by the Convention of Delegates from the United States of America & submitted to us by a Resolution of the General Court of said State passed the fourteenth Day of December last past and acknowledgeing with gratefull Hearts the goodness of the Supreme ruler of the Universe in affording the People of the United States in the Course of his Providence an Opportunity, deliberately & peaceably without fraud or surprize of entering into an Explicit and solemn compact with each other by assenting to & ratifying a new Constitution, in Order to form a more perfect Union, establish Justice, Insure domestick Tranquility, provide for the common defence, promote the general welfare and secure the Blessings of Liberty to themselves & their Posterity-Do In the Name & behalf of the People of the State of New-Hampshire assent to & ratify the said Constitution for the United States of America. And as it is the Opinion of this Convention that certain Amendments & alterations in the said Constitution would remove the fears & quiet the apprehensions of many of the good People of this State & more Effectually guard against an undue Administration of the Federal Government- The Convention do therefore recommend that the following alterations & provisions be introduced into the said Constitution.-

First That it be Explicitly declared that all Powers not expressly & particularly Delegated by the aforesaid Constitution are reserved to the several States to be, by them Exercised.-

Secondly, That there shall be one Representative to every Thirty thousand Persons according to the Census mentioned in the Constitution, untill the whole number of Representatives amount to Two hundred.-

Thirdly That Congress do not Exercise the Powers vested in them, by the fourth Section of the first Article, but in Cases when a State shall neglect or refuse to make the Regulations therein mentioned, or shall make regulations Subversive of the rights of the People to a free and equal Representation in Congress. Nor shall Congress in any Case make regulations contrary to a free and equal Representation.-

Fourthly That Congress do not lay direct Taxes but when the money arising from Impost, Excise and their other resources are insufficient for the Publick Exigencies; nor then, untill Congress shall have first made a Requisition upon the States, to Assess, Levy, & pay their respective proportions, of such requisitions agreeably to the Census fixed in the said Constitution in such way & manner as the Legislature of the State shall think best and in such Case if any State shall neglect, then Congress may Assess & Levy such States proportion together with the Interest thereon at the rate of six per Cent per Annum from the Time of payment prescribed in such requisition-

Fifthly That Congress shall erect no Company of Merchants with exclusive advantages of Commerce.-

Sixthly That no Person shall be Tryed for any Crime by which he may incur an Infamous Punishment, or loss of Life, untill he first be indicted by a Grand Jury except in such Cases as may arise in the Government and regulation of the Land & Naval Forces.-

Seventhly All Common Law Cases between Citizens of different States shall be commenced in the Common Law-Courts of the respective States & no appeal shall be allowed to the Federal Court in such Cases unless the sum or value of the thing in Controversy amount to three Thousand Dollars.-

Eighthly In Civil Actions between Citizens of different States every Issue of Fact arising in Actions at Common Law shall be Tryed by Jury, if the Parties, or either of them request it-

Ninthly-Congress shall at no Time consent that any Person holding an Office of Trust or profit under the United States shall accept any Title of Nobility or any other Title or Office from any King, Prince, or Foreign State.-

Tenth, That no standing Army shall be Kept up in time of Peace unless with the consent of three fourths of the Members of each branch of Congress, nor shall Soldiers in Time of Peace be quartered upon private Houses without the consent-of the Owners.-

Eleventh

Congress shall make no Laws touching Religion, or to infringe the rights of Conscience-

Twelfth

Congress shall never disarm any Citizen unless such as are or have been in Actual Rebellion.-

And the Convention Do. In the Name & behalf of the People of this State enjoin it upon their Representatives in Congress, at all Times untill the alterations and provisions aforesaid have been Considered agreeably to the fifth Article of the said Constitution to exert all their Influence & use all reasonable & Legal methods to obtain a ratification of the said alterations & Provisions, in such manner as is provided in the said article-And That the United States in Congress Assembled may have due notice of the assent & Ratification of the said Constitution by this Convention.-It is resolved that the Assent & Ratification aforesaid be engrossed on Parchment, together with the Recommendation & injunction aforesaid & with this Resolution-And that John Sullivan Esquire President of Convention, & John Langdon Esquire President of the State Transmit the same Countersigned by the Secretary of Convention & the Secretary of the State under their hands & Seals to the United States in Congress Assembled.-

JN° SULLIVAN presid^t of the Convention

JOHN LANGDON Presidt of State

By order

JOHN CALVE Secy of Convention

JOSEPH PEARSON Sect of State

Ratification of the Constitution by the State of New York; July 26, 1788

WE the Delegates of the People of the State of New York, duly elected and Met in Convention, having maturely considered the Constitution for the United States of America, agreed to on the seventeenth day of September, in the year One thousand Seven hundred and Eighty seven, by the Convention then assembled at Philadelphia in the Common-wealth of Pennsylvania (a Copy whereof precedes these presents) and having also seriously and deliberately considered the present situation of the United States, Do declare and make known.

That all Power is originally vested in and consequently derived from the People, and that Government is instituted by them for their common Interest Protection and Security.

That the enjoyment of Life, Liberty and the pursuit of Happiness are essential rights which every Government ought to respect and preserve.

That the Powers of Government may be reassumed by the People, whensoever it shall become necessary to their Happiness; that every Power, Jurisdiction and right, which is not by the said Constitution clearly delegated to the Congress of the United States, or the departments of the Government thereof, remains to the People of the several States, or to their respective State Governments to whom they may have granted the same; And that those Clauses in the said Constitution, which declare, that Congress shall not have or exercise certain Powers, do not imply that Congress is entitled to any Powers not given by the said Constitution; but such Clauses are to be construed either as exceptions to certain specified Powers, or as inserted merely for greater Caution.

That the People have an equal, natural and unalienable right, freely and peaceably to Exercise their Religion according to the dictates of Conscience, and that no Religious Sect or Society ought to be favoured or established by Law in preference of others.

That the People have a right to keep and bear Arms; that a well regulated Militia, including the body of the People capable of bearing Arms, is the proper, natural and safe defence of a free State;

That the Militia should not be subject to Martial Law except in time of War, Rebellion or Insurrection.

That standing Armies in time of Peace are dangerous to Liberty, and ought not to be kept up, except in Cases of necessity; and that at all times, the Military should be under strict Subordination to the civil Power.

That in time of Peace no Soldier ought to be quartered in any House without the consent of the Owner, and in time of War only by the Civil Magistrate in such manner as the Laws may direct.

That no Person ought to be taken imprisoned or disseised of his freehold, or be exiled or deprived of his Privileges, Franchises, Life, Liberty or Property but by due process of Law.

That no Person ought to be put twice in Jeopardy of Life or Limb for one and the same Offence, nor, unless in case of impeachment, be punished more than once for the same Offence.

That every Person restrained of his Liberty is entitled to an enquiry into the lawfulness of such restraint, and to a removal thereof if unlawful, and that such enquiry and removal ought not to be denied or delayed, except when on account of Public Danger the Congress shall suspend the privilege of the Writ of Habeas Corpus.

That excessive Bail ought not to be required; nor excessive Fines imposed; nor Cruel or unusual Punishments inflicted.

That (except in the Government of the Land and Naval Forces, and of the Militia when in actual Service, and in cases of Impeachment) a Presentment or Indictment by a Grand Jury ought to be observed as a necessary preliminary to the trial of all Crimes cognizable by the Judiciary of the United States, and such Trial should be speedy, public, and by an impartial Jury of the County where the Crime was committed; and that no person can be found Guilty without the unanimous consent of such Jury. But in cases of Crimes not committed within any County of any of the United States, and in Cases of Crimes committed within any County in which a general Insurrection may prevail, or which may be in the possession of a foreign Enemy, the enquiry and trial may be in such County as the Congress shall by Law direct; which County in the two Cases last mentioned should be as near as conveniently may be to that County in which the Crime may have been committed. And that in all Criminal Prosecutions, the Accused ought to be informed of the cause and nature of his Accusation, to be confronted with his accusers and the Witnesses against him, to have the means of producing his Witnesses, and the assistance of Council for his defense, and should not be compelled to give Evidence against himself.

That the trial by Jury in the extent that it obtains by the Common Law of England is one of the greatest securities to the rights of a free People, and ought to remain inviolate.

That every Freeman has a right to be secure from all unreasonable searches and seizures of his person his papers or his property, and therefore, that all Warrants to search suspected places or seize any Freeman his papers or property, without information upon Oath or Affirmation of sufficient cause, are grievous and oppressive; and that all general Warrants (or such in which the place or person suspected are not particularly designated) are dangerous and ought not to be granted.

That the People have a right peaceably to assemble together to consult for their common good, or to instruct their Representatives; and that every person has a right to Petition or apply to the Legislature for redress of Grievances.-That the Freedom of the Press ought not to be violated or restrained.

That there should be once in four years an Election of the President and Vice President, so that no Officer who may be appointed by the Congress to act as President in case of the removal, death, resignation or inability of the President and Vice President can in any case continue to act beyond the termination of the period for which the last President and Vice President were elected.

That nothing contained in the said Constitution is to be construed to prevent the Legislature of any State from passing Laws at its discretion from time to time to divide such State into convenient Districts, and to apportion its Representatives to and amongst such Districts.

That the Prohibition contained in the said Constitution against en post facto Laws, extends only to Laws concerning Crimes.

That all Appeals in Causes determineable according to the course of the common Law, ought to be by Writ of Error and not otherwise.

That the Judicial Power of the United States in cases in which a State may be a party, does not extend to criminal Prosecutions, or to authorize any Suit by any Person against a State.

That the Judicial Power of the United States as to Controversies between Citizens of the same State claiming Lands under Grants of different States is not to be construed to extend to any other Controversies between them except those which relate to such Lands, so claimed under Grants of different States.

That the Jurisdiction of the Supreme Court of the United States, or of any other Court to be instituted by the Congress, is not in any case to be encreased enlarged or extended by any Fiction Collusion or mere suggestion; And That no Treaty is to be construed so to operate as to alter the Constitution of any State.

Under these impressions and declaring that the rights aforesaid cannot be abridged or violated, and that the Explanations aforesaid are consistent with the said Constitution, And in confidence that the Amendments which shall have been proposed to the said Constitution will receive an early and mature Consideration: We the said Delegates, in the Name and in the behalf of the People of the State of New York Do by these presents Assent to and Ratify the said Constitution. In full Confidence nevertheless that until a Convention shall be called and convened for proposing Amendments to the said Constitution, the Militia of this State will not be continued in Service out of this State for a longer term than six weeks without the Consent of the Legislature thereof;-that the Congress will not make or alter any Regulation in this State respecting the times places and manner of holding Elections for Senators or Representatives unless the Legislature of this State shall neglect or refuse to make Laws or regulations for the purpose, or from any circumstance be incapable of making the same, and that in those cases such power will only be exercised until the Legislature of this State shall make provision in the Premises;-that no Excise will be imposed on any Article of the Growth production or Manufacture of the United States, or any of them within this State, Ardent Spirits excepted; And that the Congress will not lay direct Taxes within this State, but when the Monies arising from the Impost and Excise shall be insufficient for the public Exigencies, nor then, until Congress shall first have made a Requisition upon this State to assess levy and pay the Amount of such Requisition made agreably to the Census fixed in the said Constitution in such way and manner as the Legislature of this State shall judge best, but that in such case, if the State shall neglect or refuse to pay its proportion pursuant to such Requisition, then the Congress may assess and levy this States proportion together with Interest at the Rate of six per Centum per Annum from the time at which the same was required to be paid.

Done in Convention at Poughkeepsie in the County of Dutchess in the State of New York the twenty sixth day of July in the year of our I'ord One thousand Seven hundred and Eighty eight.

By Order of the Convention.
GEO: CLINTON President
Attested
JOHN McKESSON
ABM B. BANCKER Secretaries-

AND the Convention do in the Name and Behalf of the People of the State of New York enjoin it upon their Representatives in the Congress, to Exert all their Influence, and use all reasonable means to Obtain a Ratification of the following Amendments to the said Constitution in the manner prescribed therein; and in all Laws to be passed by the Congress in the meantime to conform to the spirit of the said Amendments as far as the Constitution will admit.

That there shall be one Representative for every thirty thousand Inhabitants, according to the enumeration or Census mentioned in the Constitution, until the whole number of Representatives amounts to two hundred; after which that number shall be continued or encreased but not diminished, as Congress shall direct, and according to such ratio as the Congress shall fix, in conformity to the rule prescribed for the Apportionment of Representatives and direct Taxes.

That the Congress do not impose any Excise on any Article (except Ardent Spirits) of the Growth Production or Manufacture of the United States, or any of them.

That Congress do not lay direct Taxes but when the Monies arising from the Impost and Excise shall be insufficient for the Public Exigencies. nor then until Congress shall first have made a Requisition upon the States to assess levy and pay their respective proportions of such Requisition, agreably to the Census fixed in the said Constitution, in such way and manner as the Legislatures of the respective States shall judge best; and in such Case, if any State shall neglect or refuse to pay its proportion pursuant to such Requisition, then Congress may assess and levy such States proportion, together with Interest at the rate of six per C`entum per Annum, from the time of Payment prescribed in such Requisition.

That the Congress shall not make or alter any Regulation in any State respecting the times places and manner of holding Elections for Senators or Representatives, unless the Legislature of such State shall neglect or refuse to make Laws or Regulations for the purpose, or from any circumstance be incapable of making the same; and then only until the Legislature of such State shall make provision in the premises; provided that Congress may prescribe the time for the Election of Representatives.

That no Persons except natural born Citizens, or such as were Citizens on or before the fourth day of July one thousand seven hundred and seventy six, or such as held Commissions under the United States during the War, and have at any time since the fourth day of July one thousand seven hundred and seventy six become Citizens of one or other of the United States, and who shall be Freeholders, shall be eligible to the Places of President, Vice President, or Members of either House of the Congress of the United States.

That the Congress do not grant Monopolies or erect any Company with exclusive Advantages of Commerce.

That no standing Army or regular Troops shall be raised or kept up in time of peace, without the consent of two-thirds of the Senators and Representatives present, in each House.

That no Money be borrowed on the Credit of the United States without the Assent of two-thirds of the Senators and Representatives present in each House.

That the Congress shall not declare War Without the concurrence of two-thirds of the Senators and Representatives present in each House.

That the Privilege of the Habeas Corpus shall not by any Law be suspended for a longer term than six Months, or until twenty days after the Meeting of the Congress next following the passing of the Act for such suspension.

That the Right of the Congress to exercise exclusive Legislation over such District, not exceeding ten Miles square, as may by cession of a particular State, and the acceptance of Congress, become the Seat of the Government of the United States, shall not be so exercised, as to exempt the Inhabitants of such District from paying the like Taxes Imposts Duties and Excises, as shall be imposed on the other Inhabitants of the State in which such District may be; and that no person shall be privileged within the said District from Arrest for Crimes committed, or Debts contracted out of the said District.

That the Right of exclusive Legislation with respect to such places as may be purchased for the Erection of Forts, Magazines, Arsenals, Dockyards and other needful Buildings, shall not authorize the Congress to make any Law to prevent the Laws of the States respectively in which they may be, from extending to such places in ail civil and Criminal Matters except as to such Persons as shall be in the Service of the United States; nor to them witl respect to Crimes committed without such Places.

That the Compensation for the Senators and Representatives be ascertained by standing Laws; and that no alteration of the existing rate of Compensation shall operate for the Benefit of the Representatives, until after a subsequent Election shall have been had.

That the Journals of the Congress shall be published at least once a year, with the exception of such parts relating to Treaties or Military operations, as in the Judgment of either House shall require Secrecy; and that both Houses of Congress shall always keep their Doors open during their Sessions, unless the Business may in their Opinion requires Secrecy. That the yeas & nays shall be entered on the Journals whenever two Members in either House may require it.

That no Capitation Tax shall ever be laid by the Congress.

That no Person be eligible as a Senator for more than six years in any term of twelve years; and that the Legislatures of the respective States may recal their Senators or either of them, and elect others in their stead, to serve the remainder of the time for which the Senators so recalled were appointed.

That no Senator or Representative shall during the time for which he was elected be appointed to any Office under the Authority of the United States.

That the Authority given to the Executives of the States to fill the vacancies of Senators be abolished, and that such vacancies be filled by the respective Legislatures.

That the Power of Congress to pass uniform Laws concerning Bankruptcy shall only extend to Merchants and other Traders; and that the States respectively may pass Laws for the relief of other Insolvent Debtors.

That no Person shall be eligible to the Office of President of the United States a third time.

That the Executive shall not grant Pardons for Treason, unless with the Consent of the Congress; but may at his discretion grant

Reprieves to persons convicted of Treason, until their Cases, can be laid before the Congress.

That the President or person exercising his Powers for the time being, shall not command an Army in the Field in person, without the previous desire of the Congress.

That all Letters Patent, Commissions, Pardons, Writs and Process of the United States, shall run in the Name of the People of the United States, and be tested in the Name of the President of the United States, or the person exercising his powers for the time being, or the first Judge of the Court out of which the same shall issue, as the case may be.

That the Congress shall not constitute ordain or establish any Tribunals or Inferior Courts, with any other than Appellate Jurisdiction, except such as may be necessary for the Tryal of Causes of Admiralty and Maritime Jurisdiction, and for the Trial of Piracies and Felonies committed on the High Seas; and in all other Cases to which the Judicial Power of the United States extends, and in which the Supreme Court of the United States has not original Jurisdiction, the Causes shall be heard tried, and determined in some one of the State Courts, with the right of Appeal to the Supreme Court of the United States, or other proper Tribunal to be established for that purpose by the Congress, with such exceptions, and under such regulations as the Congress shall make.

That the Court for the Trial of Impeachments shall consist of the Senate, the Judges of the Supreme Court of the United States, and the first or Senior Judge for the time being, of the highest Court of general and ordinary common Law Jurisdiction in each State;-that the Congress shall by standing Laws designate the Courts in the respective States answering this Description, and in States having no Courts exactly answering this Description, shall designate some other Court, preferring such if any there be, whose Judge or Judges may hold their places during good Behaviour-

Provided that no more than one Judge, other than Judges of the Supreme Court of the United States, shall come from one State- That the Congress be authorized to pass Laws for compensating the said

Judges for such Services and for compelling their Attendance- and that a Majority at least of the said Judges shall be requisite to constitute the said Court-that no person impeached shall sit as a Member thereof. That each Member shall previous to the entering upon any Trial take an Oath or Affirmation, honestly and impartially to hear and determine the Cause-and that a Majority of the Members present shall be necessary to a Conviction.

That persons aggrieved by any Judgment, Sentence or Decree of the Supreme Court of the United States, in any Cause in which that Court has original Jurisdiction, with such exceptions and under such Regulations as the Congress shall make concerning the same, shall upon application, have a Commission to be issued by the President of the United States, to such Men learned in the Law as he shall nominate, and by and with the Advice and consent of the Senate appoint, not less than seven, authorizing such Commissioners, or any seven or more of them, to correct the Errors in such Judgment or to review such Sentence and Decree, as the case may be, and to do Justice to the parties in the Premises.

That no Judge of the Supreme Court of the United States shall hold any other Office under the United States, or any of them.

That the Judicial Power of the United States shall extend to no Controversies respecting Land, unless it relate to Claims of Territory or Jurisdiction between States, or to Claims of Land between Individuals, or between States and Individuals under the Grants of different States.

That the Militia of any State shall not be compelled to serve without the limits of the State for a longer term than six weeks, without the Consent of the Legislature thereof.

That the words without the Consent of the Congress in the seventh Clause of the ninth Section of the first Article of the Constitution, be expunged.

That the Senators and Representatives and all Executive and Judicial Officers of the United States shall be bound by Oath or Affirmation not to infringe or violate the Constitutions or Rights of the respective States.

That the Legislatures of the respective States may make Provision by Law, that the Electors of the Election Districts to be by them appointed shall chuse a Citizen of the United States who shall have been an Inhabitant of such District for the Term of one year immediately proceeding the time of his Election, for one of the Representatives of such State.

Done in Convention at Poughkeepsie in the County of Dutchess in the State of New York the twenty sixth day of July in the year of our Lord One thousand seven hundred and Eighty eight.

By Order of the Convention.

Attested- GEO: CLINTON President

Ratification of the Constitution by the
State of Rhode Island; May 29, 1790

Ratification of the Constitution, by the Convention of the State of Rhode-Island and Providence Plantations.

We the Delegates of the People of the State of Rhode-Island, and Providence Plantations, duly elected and met in Convention, having maturely considered the Constitution for the United States of America, agreed to on the seventeenth day of September, in the year one thousand seven hundred and eighty seven, by the Convention then assembled at Philadelphia, in the Commonwealth of Pennsylvania (a Copy whereof precedes these presents) and having also seriously and deliberately considered the present situation of this State, do declare and make known:

In That there are certain natural rights, of which men when they form a social compact, cannot deprive or divest their posterity, among which are the enjoyment of Life and Liberty, with the means of acquiring, possessing and protecting Property, and pursuing and obtaining happiness and safety.

2d That all power is naturally vested in, and consequently derived from the People; that magistrates therefore are their trustees and agents, and at all times amenable to them.

3d That the powers of government may be reassumed by the people, whensoever it shall become necessary to their happiness:- That the rights of the States respectively, to nominate and appoint all State Officers, and every other power, jurisdiction and right, which is not by the said constitution clearly delegated to the Congress of the United States or to the departments of government thereof, remain to the people of the several states, or their respective State Governments to whom they may have granted the same; and that those clauses in the said constitution which declare that Congress shall not have or exercise certain powers, do not imply, that Congress is entitled to any powers not given by the said constitution, but such clauses are to be construed as exceptions to certain specified powers, or as inserted merely for greater caution.

4th That religion, or the duty which we owe to our Creator, and the manner of discharging it, can be directed only by reason and conviction, and not by force or violence, and therefore all men, have an equal, natural and unalienable right to the free exercise of religion, according to the dictates of conscience, and that no particular religious sect or society ought to be favoured, or established by law in preference to others.

5th That the legislative, executive and judiciary powers of government, should be separate and distinct, and that the members of the two first may be restrained from oppression, by feeling and participating the publick burthens, they should at fixed periods be reduced to a private station, return into the mass of the people, and the vacancies be supplied by certain and regular elections, in which all, or any part of the former members, to be eligible or ineligible, as the rules of the constitution of government and the laws shall direct.

6th That elections of representatives in legislature ought to be free and frequent, and all men having sufficient evidence of permanent common interest with, and attachment to the community ought to have the right of suffrage, and no aid, charge tax or fee can be set, rated or levied upon the people, without their own consent or that of their representatives so elected, nor can they be bound by any law, to which they have not in like manner assented for the publick good.

7th That all power of suspending laws or the execution of laws, by any authority without the consent of the representatives of the people in the legislature, is injurious to their rights, and ought not to be exercised.

8th That in all capital and criminal prosecutions, a man hath a right to demand the cause and nature of his accusation, to be confronted with the accusers and witnesses, to call for evidence and be allowed counsel in his favour, and to a fair and speedy trial by an impartial jury of his vicinage, without whose unanimous consent he cannot be found guilty; (except in the government of the land and naval forces) nor can he be compelled to give evidence against himself.

9th That no freeman ought to be taken, imprisoned or disseised of his freehold, liberties, privileges, or franchises, or outlawed, or exiled, or in any manner destroyed or deprived of his life, liberty or property but by the trial by jury, or by the law of the land.

10th That every freeman restrained of his liberty, is intitled to a remedy, to enquire into the lawfulness thereof, and to remove the same if unlawful, and that such remedy ought not to be denied or delayed.

11th That in controversies respecting property, and in suits between man and man the antient trial by jury, as bath been exercised by us and our ancestors, from the time whereof the memory of man is not to the contrary, is one of the greatest securities to the rights of the people, and ought to remain sacred and inviolate.

12th That every freeman ought to obtain right and justice, freely and without sale, completely and without denial, promptly and without delay, and that all establishments or regulations contravening these rights, are oppressive and unjust.

13th That excessive bail ought not to be required, nor excessive fines imposed, nor cruel or unusual punishments inflicted.

14th That every person has a right to be secure from all unreasonable searches and seisures of his person, his papers or his property, and therefore that all warrants to search suspected places or seise any person, his papers or his property, without information upon oath, or affirmation, of sufficient cause, are grievous and oppressive, and that all general warrants for such in which the place or person suspected, are not particularly designated,) are dangerous, and ought not to be granted.

15th That the people have a right peaceably to assemble together, to consult for their common good, or to instruct their representatives; and that every person has a right to petition or apply to the legislature for redress of grievances.

16th That the people have a right to freedom of speech and of writing, and publishing their sentiments, that freedom of the press is one of the greatest bulwarks of liberty, and ought not to be violated.

17th That the people have a right to keep and bear arms, that a well regulated militia, including the body of the people capable of bearing arms, is the proper, natural and safe defence of a free state; that the militia shall not be subject to martial law except in time of war, rebellion or insurrection; that standing armies in time of peace, are dangerous to liberty, and ought not to be kept up, except in cases of necessity; and that at all times the military should be under strict subordination to the civil power; that in time of peace no soldier ought to be quartered in any house, without the consent of the owner, and in time of war, only by the civil magistrate, in such manner as the law directs.

18th That any person religiously scrupulous of bearing arms, ought to be exempted, upon payment of an equivalent, to employ another to bear arms in his stead.

Under these impressions, and declaring, that the rights aforesaid cannot be abridged or violated, and that the explanations aforesaid, are consistent with the said constitution, and in confidence that the Amendments hereafter mentioned, will receive an early and mature consideration, and conformably to the fifth article of said constitution, speedily become a part thereof; We the said delegates, in the name, and in the behalf of the People, of the State of Rhode-Island and Providence-Plantations, do by these Presents, assent to, and ratify the said Constitution. In full confidence nevertheless, that until the Amendments hereafter proposed and undermentioned shall be agreed to and ratified, pursuant to the aforesaid fifth article, the militia of this State will not be continued in service out of this State for a longer term than six weeks, without the consent of the legislature thereof; That the Congress will not make or alter any regulation in this State, respecting the times, places and manner of holding elections for senators or representatives, unless the legislature of this state shall neglect, or refuse to make laws or regulations for the purpose, or from any circumstance be incapable of making the same; and that n those cases, such power will only be exercised, until the legislature of this State shall make provision in the Premises, that the Congress will not lay direct taxes within this State, but when the monies arising from the Impost, Tonnage and Excise shall be insufficient for the publick exigencies, nor until the Congress shall have first made a requisition upon this State to assess, levy and pay the amount of such requisition, made agreeable to the census fixed in the said constitution, in such way and manner, as the legislature of this State shall judge best, and that the Congress will not lay any capitation or poll tax.

Done in Convention, at Newport in the County of Newport, in the State of Rhode-Island and Providence-Plantations, the twenty ninth day of May, in the Year of our Lord one thousand seven hundred and ninety, and in the fourteenth year of the Independence of the United

States of America.
By order of the Convention,
DANIEL OWEN President
Attest, DANIEL UPDIKE Secty

And the Convention, do in the name and behalf of the People of the State of Rhode-Island and Providence Plantations, enjoin it upon their Senators and Representative or Representatives, which may be elected to represent this State in Congress, to exert all their influence, and use all reasonable means to obtain a ratification of the following Amendments to the said Constitution, in the manner prescribed therein, and in all laws to be passed by the Congress in the mean time, to conform to the spirit of the said Amendments, as far as the constitution will admit.

Amendments
1st The United States shall guarantee to each State its sovereignty, freedom and independence, and every power, jurisdiction and right, which is not by this constitution expressly delegated to the United States.
2d That Congress shall not alter, modify or interfere in the times, places or manner of holding elections for Senators and Representatives, or either of them, except when the legislature of any state shall neglect, refuse or be disabled by invasion or rebellion to prescribe the same; or in case when the provision made by the states, is so imperfect as that no consequent election is had, and then only until the legislature of such state, shall make provision in the premises.
3d It is declared by the Convention, that the judicial power of the United States, in cases in which a state may be a party, does not extend to criminal prosecutions, or to authorize any suit by any person against a State; but to remove all doubts or controversies respecting the same, that it be especially expressed as a part of the constitution of the United States, that Congress shall not directly or indirectly, either by themselves or through the judiciary, interfere with any one of the states, in the redemption of paper money already emitted and now in circulation, or in liquidating or discharging the publick securities of any one state: that each and every state shall have the

exclusive right of making such laws and regulations for the before mentioned purpose, as they shall think proper.

4th That no Amendments to the constitution of the United States hereafter to be made, pursuant to the fifth article, shall take effect, or become a part of the constitution of the United States after the Year one thousand seven hundred and ninety three, without the consent of eleven of the states, heretofore united under one confederation.

5th That the judicial powers of the United States shall extend to no possible case, where the cause of action shall have originated before the ratification of this constitution, except in disputes between states about their territory, disputes between persons claiming lands under grants of different states, and debts due to the United States.

6th That no person shall be compelled to do military duty, otherwise than by voluntary enlistment, except in cases of general invasion; any thing in the second paragraph of the sixth article of the constitution, or any law made under the constitution to the contrary notwithstanding.

7th That no capitation or poll-tax shall ever be laid by Congress.

8th In cases of direct taxes, Congress shall first make requisitions on the several states to assess, levy and pay their respective proportions of such requisitions, in such way and manner, as the legislatures of the several states shall judge best; and in case any state shall neglect or refuse to pay its proportion pursuant to such requisition, then Congress may assess and levy such state's proportion, together with interest at the rate of six per cent. per annum, from the time prescribed in such requisition.

9th That Congress shall lay no direct taxes, without the consent of the legislatures of three fourths of the states in the Union.

10th That the journals of the proceedings of the Senate and house of Representatives shall be published as soon as conveniently may be, at least once in every year, except such parts thereof relating to treaties, alliances or military operations, as in their judgment require secrecy.

11th That regular statements of the receipts and expenditures of all publick monies, shall be published at least once a year.

12th As standing armies in time of peace are dangerous to liberty and ought not to be kept up, except in cases of necessity; and as at all times the military should be under strict subordination to the civil power, that therefore no standing army, or regular toops shall be raised, or kept up in time of peace.

13th That no monies be borrowed on the credit of the United States without the assent of two thirds of the Senators and Representatives present in each house.

14th That the Congress shall not declare war, without the concurrence of two thirds of the Senators and Representatives present in each house.

15th That the words " without the consent of Congress " in the seventh clause in the ninth section of the first article of the constitution be expunged.

16th That no judge of the supreme court of the United States, shall hold any other office under the United States, or any of them; nor shall any officer appointed by Congress, or by the President and Senate of the United States, be permitted to hold any office under the appointment of any of the states.

17th As a traffick tending to establish or continue the slavery of any part of the human species, is disgraceful to the cause of liberty and humanity, that Congress shall, as soon as may be, promote and establish such laws and regulations, as may effectually prevent the importation of slaves of very description into the United States.

18th That the State Legislatures have power to recall, when they think it expedient, their federal senators, and to send others in their stead.

19th That Congress have power to establish a uniform rule of inhabitancy, or settlement of the poor of the different States throughout the United States.

20th That Congress erect no company with exclusive advantages of commerce.

21st That when two members shall move or call for the ayes and nays on any question, they shall be entered on the journals of the houses respectively.

Done in Convention at Newport, in the County of Newport in the State of Rhode-Island and Providence Plantations, the twenty ninth day of May, in the year of our Lord one thousand seven hundred and

ninety, and the fourteenth year of the independence of the United States of America. By order of the Convention,
DANIEL OWEN President.
Attest DANIEL UPDIKE. Secty.

Ratification of the Constitution by the
State of South Carolina; May 23, 1788

In Convention of the people of the state of South Carolina by their Representatives held in the city of Charleston on Monday the twelfth day of May and continued by divers Adjournments to friday the twenty third day of May Anno Domini One thousand seven hundred and eighty eight, and in the twelfth Year of the Independence of the United States of America.

The Convention having maturely considered the constitution or form of Government reported to Congress by the Convention of Delegates from the United states of America and submitted to them by a Resolution of the Legislature of this State passed the seventeenth and eighteenth days of February last in order to form a more perfect Union, establish Justice, ensure Domestic tranquillity, provide for the common defence, promote the general Welfare and secure the blessings of Liberty to the people of the said United States and their posterity DO in the name and behalf of the people of this State hereby assent to and ratify the said Constitution.

Done in Convention the twenty third day of May in the Year of our Lord One thousand seven hundred and eighty eight, and of the Independence of the United States of America the twelfth.-

THOMAS PINCKNEY
President Attest
JOHN SANDFORD DART
Secretary

And Whereas it is essential to the preservation of the rights reserved to the several states, and the freedom of the people under the operations of a General government that the right of prescribing the manner time and places of holding the Elections to the Federal Legislature, should be for ever inseparably annexed to the sovereignty of the several states. This convention doth declare that the same ought to remain to all posterity a perpetual and fundamental right in the local, exclusive of the interference of the General Government except in cases where the Legislatures of the States, shall refuse or neglect to perform and fulfil the same according to the tenor of the said Constitution.

This Convention doth also declare that no Section or paragraph of the said Constitution warrants a Construction that the states do not retain every power not expressly relinquished by them and vested in the General Government of the Union.

Resolved that the general Government of the United States ought never to impose direct taxes, but where the monies arising from the duties, imposts and excise are insufficient for the public exigencies nor then until Congress shall have made a requisition upon the states to Assess levy and pay their respective proportions of such requisitions And in case any state shall neglect or refuse to pay its proportion pursuant to such requisition then Congress may assess and levy such state's proportion together with Interest thereon at the rate of six per centum per annum from the time of payment prescribed by such requisition-

Resolved that the third section of the Sixth Article ought to be amended by inserting the word " other " between the words " *no* " and " *religious* "

Resolved that it be a standing instruction to all such delegates as may hereafter be elected to represent this State in the general Government to exert their utmost abilities and influence to effect an Alteration of the Constitution conformably to the foregoing Resolutions.

Done in Convention the twenty third day of May in the year of our Lord One thousand Seven hundred and eighty eight and of the Independence of the United States of America the twelfth THOMAS PINCKNEY

President Attest

JOHN SANFORD DART

Secretary

Ratification of the Constitution by the State of Virginia; June 26, 1788.

Virginia to wit

We the Delegates of the People of Virginia duly elected in pursuance of a recommendation from the General Assembly and now met in Convention having fully and freely investigated and discussed the proceedings of the Federal Convention and being prepared as well as the most mature deliberation hath enabled us to decide thereon Do in the name and in behalf of the People of Virginia declare and make known that the powers granted under the Constitution being derived from the People of the United States may be resumed by them whensoever the same shall be perverted to their injury or oppression and that every power not granted thereby remains with them and at their will: that therefore no right of any denomination can be cancelled abridged restrained or modified by the Congress by the Senate or House of Representatives acting in any Capacity by the President or any Department or Officer of the United States except in those instances in which power is given by the Constitution for those purposes: & that among other essential rights the liberty of Conscience and of the Press cannot be cancelled abridged restrained or modified by any authority of the United States. With these impressions with a solemn appeal to the Searcher of hearts for the purity of our intentions and under the conviction that whatsoever imperfections may exist in the Constitution ought rather to be examined in the mode prescribed therein than to bring the Union into danger by a delay with a hope of obtaining Amendments previous to the Ratification, We the said Delegates in the name and in behalf of the People of Virginia do by these presents assent to and ratify the Constitution recommended on the seventeenth day of September one thousand seven hundred and eighty seven by the Federal Convention for the Government of the United States hereby announcing to all those whom it may concern that the said Constitution is binding upon the said People according to an authentic Copy hereto annexed in the Words following; .

Done in Convention this twenty Sixth day of June one thousand

seven hundred and eighty eight
By Order of the Convention
EDM^D PENDLETON President

Virginia to wit:

Subsequent Amendments agreed to in Convention as necessary to the proposed Constitution of Government for the United States, recommended to the consideration of the Congress which shall first assemble under the said Constitution to be acted upon according to the mode prescribed in the fifth article thereof:

Videlicet;

That there be a Declaration or Bill of Rights asserting and securing from encroachment the essential and unalienable Rights of the People in some such manner as the following;

First, That there are certain natural rights of which men, when they form a social compact cannot deprive or divest their posterity, among which are the enjoyment of life and liberty, with the means of acquiring, possessing and protecting property, and pursuing and obtaining happiness and safety.

Second. That all power is naturally vested in and consequently derived from the people; that Magistrates, therefore, are their trustees and agents and at all times amenable to them.

Third, That Government ought to be instituted for the common benefit, protection and security of the People; and that the doctrine of non-resistance against arbitrary power and oppression is absurd slavish, and destructive of the good and happiness of mankind.

Fourth, That no man or set of Men are entitled to exclusive or seperate public emoluments or privileges from the community, but in Consideration of public services; which not being descendible, neither ought the offices of Magistrate, Legislator or Judge, or any other public office to be hereditary.

Fifth, That the legislative, executive, and judiciary powers of Government should be seperate and distinct, and that the members of the two first may be restrained from oppression by feeling and participating the public burthens, they should, at fixt periods be reduced to a private station, return into the mass of the people; and the vacancies be supplied by certain and regular elections; in which all or any part of the former members to be elegible or ineligible, as the rules of the Constitution of Government, and the laws shall direct.

Sixth, That elections of representatives in the legislature ought to be free and frequent, and all men having sufficient evidence of permanent common interest with and attachment to the Community ought to have the right of suffrage: and no aid, charge, tax or fee can be set, rated, or levied upon the people without their own consent, or that of their representatives so elected, nor can they be bound by any law to which they have not in like manner assented for the public good.

Seventh, That all power of suspending laws or the execution of laws by any authority, without the consent of the representatives of the people in the legislature is injurious to their rights, and ought not to be exercised.

Eighth, That in all capital and criminal prosecutions, a man hath a right to demand the cause and nature of his accusation, to be confronted with the accusers and witnesses, to call for evidence and be allowed counsel in his favor, and to a fair and speedy trial by an impartial Jury of his vicinage, without whose unanimous consent he cannot be found guilty, (except in the government of the land and naval forces) nor can he be compelled to give evidence against himself.

Ninth. That no freeman ought to be taken, imprisoned, or disseised of his freehold, liberties, privileges or franchises, or outlawed or exiled, or in any manner destroyed or deprived of his life, liberty or property but by the law of the land.

Tenth. That every freeman restrained of his liberty is entitled to a remedy to enquire into the lawfulness thereof, and to remove the same, if unlawful, and that such remedy ought not to be denied nor delayed.

Eleventh. That in controversies respecting property, and in suits between man and man, the ancient trial by Jury is one of the greatest Securities to the rights of the people, and ought to remain sacred and inviolable.

Twelfth. That every freeman ought to find a certain remedy by recourse to the laws for all injuries and wrongs he may receive in his person, property or character. He ought to obtain right and justice freely without sale, compleatly and without denial, promptly and without delay, and that all establishments or regulations contravening these rights, are oppressive and unjust.

Thirteenth, That excessive Bail ought not be required, nor excessive fines imposed, nor cruel and unusual punishments inflicted.

Fourteenth, That every freeman has a right to be secure from all unreasonable searches and siezures of his person, his papers and his property; all warrants, therefore, to search suspected places, or sieze any freeman, his papers or property, without information upon Oath (or affirmation of a person religiously scrupulous of taking an oath) of legal and sufficient cause, are grievous and oppressive; and all general Warrants to search suspected places, or to apprehend any suspected person, without specially naming or describing the place or person, are dangerous and ought not to be granted.

Fifteenth, That the people have a right peaceably to assemble together to consult for the common good, or to instruct their Representatives; and that every freeman has a right to petition or apply to the legislature for redress of grievances.

Sixteenth, That the people have a right to freedom of speech, and of writing and publishing their Sentiments; but the freedom of the press is one of the greatest bulwarks of liberty and ought not to be violated.

Seventeenth, That the people have a right to keep and bear arms; that a well regulated Militia composed of the body of the people trained to arms is the proper, natural and safe defence of a free State. That standing armies in time of peace are dangerous to liberty, and therefore ought to be avoided, as far as the circumstances and protection of the Community will admit; and that in all cases the military should be under strict subordination to and governed by the Civil power.

Eighteenth, That no Soldier in time of peace ought to be quartered in any house without the consent of the owner, and in time of war in such manner only as the laws direct.

Nineteenth, That any person religiously scrupulous of bearing arms ought to be exempted upon payment of an equivalent to employ another to bear arms in his stead.

Twentieth, That religion or the duty which we owe to our Creator, and the manner of discharging it can be directed only by reason and conviction, not by force or violence, and therefore all men have an equal, natural and unalienable right to the free exercise of religion according to the dictates of conscience, and that no particular religious sect or society ought to be favored or established by Law in preference to others.

Amendments TO THE BODY OF THE CONSTITUTION

First, That each State in the Union shall respectively retain every power, jurisdiction and right which is not by this Constitution delegated to the Congress of the United States or to the departments of the Federal Government.

Second, That there shall be one representative for every thirty thousand, according to the Enumeration or Census mentioned in the Constitution, until the whole number of representatives amounts to two hundred; after which that number shall be continued or encreased as the Congress shall direct, upon the principles fixed by the Constitution by apportioning the Representatives of each State to some greater number of people from time to time as population encreases.

Third, When Congress shall lay direct taxes or excises, they shall immediately inform the Executive power of each State of the quota of such state according to the Census herein directed, which is proposed to be thereby raised; And if the Legislature of any State shall pass a law which shall be effectual for raising such quota at the time required by Congress, the taxes and excises laid by Congress shall not be collected, in such State.

Fourth, That the members of the Senate and House of Representatives shall be ineligible to, and incapable of holding, any civil office under the authority of the United States, during the time for which they shall respectively be elected.

Fifth, That the Journals of the proceedings of the Senate and House of Representatives shall be published at least once in every year, except such parts thereof relating to treaties, alliances or military operations, as in their judgment require secrecy.

Sixth, That a regular statement and account of the receipts and expenditures of all public money shall be published at least once in every year.

Seventh, That no commercial treaty shall be ratified without the concurrence of two thirds of the whole number of the members of the Senate; and no Treaty ceding, contracting, restraining or suspending the territorial rights or claims of the United States, or any of them or their, or any of their rights or claims to fishing in the American seas, or navigating the American rivers shall be but in cases of the most urgent and extreme necessity, nor shall any such treaty be ratified without the concurrence of three fourths of the whole number of the members of both houses respectively.

Eighth, That no navigation law, or law regulating Commerce shall be passed without the consent of two thirds of the Members present in both houses.

Ninth, That no standing army or regular troops shall be raised or kept up in time of peace, without the consent of two thirds of the members present in both houses.

Tenth, That no soldier shall be inlisted for any longer term than four years, except in time of war, and then for no longer term than the continuance of the war.

Eleventh, That each State respectively shall have the power to provide for organizing, arming and disciplining it's own Militia, whensoever Congress shall omit or neglect to provide for the same. That the Militia shall not be subject to Martial law, except when in actual service in time of war, invasion, or rebellion; and when not in the actual service of the United States, shall be subject only to such fines, penalties and punishments as shall be directed or inflicted by the laws of its own State.

Twelfth That the exclusive power of legislation given to Congress over the Federal Town and its adjacent District and other places purchased or to be purchased by Congress of any of the States shall extend only to such regulations as respect the police and good government thereof.

Thirteenth, That no person shall be capable of being President of the United States for more than eight years in any term of sixteen years.

Fourteenth That the judicial power of the United States shall be vested in one supreme Court, and in such courts of Admiralty as Congress may from time to time ordain and establish in any of the different States: The Judicial power shall extend to all cases in Law and Equity arising under treaties made, or which shall be made under the authority of the United States; to all cases affecting ambassadors other foreign ministers and consuls; to all cases of Admiralty and maritime jurisdiction; to controversies to which the United States shall be a party; to controversies between two or States, and between parties claiming lands under the grants of different States. In all cases affecting ambassadors, other foreign ministers and Consuls, and those in which a State shall be a party, the supreme court shall have original jurisdiction; in all other cases before mentioned the supreme Court shall have appellate jurisdiction as to matters of law only: except in cases of equity, and of admiralty and maritime jurisdiction, in which the Supreme Court shall have appellate jurisdiction both as to law and fact, with such exceptions and under such regulations as the Congress shall make. But the judicial power of the United States shall extend to no case where the cause of action shall have originated before the ratification of this Constitution; except in disputes between States about their Territory, disputes between persons claiming lands under the grants of different States, and suits for debts due to the United States.

Fifteenth, That in criminal prosecutions no man shall be restrained in the exercise of the usual and accustomed right of challenging or excepting to the Jury.

Sixteenth, That Congress shall not alter, modify or interfere in the times, places, or manner of holding elections for Senators and Representatives or either of them, except when the legislature of any State shall neglect, refuse or be disabled by invasion or rebellion to prescribe the same.

Seventeenth, That those clauses which declare that Congress shall not exercise certain powers be not interpreted in any manner whatsoever to extend the powers of Congress. But that they may be construed either as making exceptions to the specified powers where this shall be the case, or otherwise as inserted merely for greater caution.

Eighteenth, That the laws ascertaining the compensation to Senators and Representatives for their services be postponed in their operation, until after the election of Representatives immediately succeeding the passing thereof; that excepted, which shall first be passed on the Subject.

Nineteenth, That some Tribunal other than the Senate be provided for trying impeachments of Senators.

Twentieth, That the Salary of a Judge shall not be encreased or diminished during his continuance in Office, otherwise than by general regulations of Salary which may take place on a revision of the subject at stated periods of not less than seven years to commence from the time such Salaries shall be first ascertained by Congress. And the Convention do, in the name and behalf of the People of this Commonwealth enjoin it upon their Representatives in Congress to exert all their influence and use all reasonable and legal methods to obtain a Ratification of the foregoing alterations and provisions in the manner provided by the fifth article of the said Constitution; and in all Congressional laws to be passed in the mean time, to conform to the spirit of those Amendments as far as the said Constitution will admit.

Done in Convention this twenty seventh day of June in the year of our Lord one thousand seven hundred and eighty eight.

By order of the Convention.

EDM^D PENDLETON President

Appendix D: Bill Of Rights in Some Original State Constitutions

BILL OF RIGHTS OF SELECTED ORIGINAL STATE CONSTITUTIONS

All of the original thirteen states had written Constitutions in place before the U.S. Constitution was written. Most state Constitutions included a declaration of rights. Extracts from three states, Pennsylvania, North Carolina and Maryland, are provided, in no particular order.

Constitution of Pennsylvania : September 28, 1776

WHEREAS all government ought to be instituted and supported for the security and protection of the community as such, and to enable the individuals who compose it to enjoy their natural rights, and the other blessings which the Author of existence has bestowed upon man; and whenever these great ends of government are not obtained, the people have a right, by common consent to change it, and take such measures as to them may appear necessary to promote their safety and happiness. AND WHEREAS the inhabitants o f this commonwealth have in consideration of protection only, heretofore acknowledged allegiance to the king of Great Britain; and the said king has not only withdrawn that protection, but commenced, and still continues to carry on, with unabated vengeance, a most cruel and unjust war against them, employing therein, not only the troops of Great Britain, but foreign mercenaries, savages and slaves, for the avowed purpose of reducing them to a total and abject submission to the despotic domination of the British parliament, with many other acts of tyranny, (more fully set forth in the declaration of Congress) whereby all allegiance and fealty to the said king and his successors, are dissolved and at an end, and all power and authority derived from him ceased in these colonies. AND WHEREAS it is absolutely necessary for the welfare and safety of the inhabitants of said colonies, that they be henceforth free and independent States, and that just, permanent, and proper forms of government exist in every part of them, derived from and founded on the authority of the people only, agreeable to the directions of the honourable American Congress. We, the representatives of the freemen of Pennsylvania, in general convention met, for the express purpose of framing such a government, confessing the goodness of the great Governor of the universe (who alone knows to what degree of earthly happiness mankind mav attain, by perfecting the arts of government) in permitting the people of this State, by common consent, and without violence, deliberately to form for themselves such just rules as they shall think best, for governing their future society, and being fully convinced, that itis our indispensable duty to establish such original principles of government, as will best promote the general happiness of the people of this State, and their posterity, and provide for future improvements, without partiality for, or prejudice against any particular class, sect, or denomination of men whatever, do, by virtue of the authority vested in use by our constituents, ordain, declare, and establish, the following Declaration of Rights and Frame of Government, to be the CONSTITUTION of this commonwealth, and to remain in force therein for ever, unaltered, except in such articles as shall hereafter on experience be found to require improvement, and which shall by the same authority of the people, fairly delegated as this frame of government directs, be amended or improved for the more effectual obtaining and securing the great end and design of all government, herein before mentioned.

A DECLARATION OF THE RIGHTS OF THE INHABITANTS OF THE COMMONWEALTH OR STATE OF PENNSYLVANIA

I. That all men are born equally free and independent, and have certain natural, inherent and inalienable rights, amongst which are, the enjoying and defending life and liberty, acquiring, possessing and protecting property, and pursuing and obtaining happiness and safety.

II. That all men have a natural and unalienable right to worship Almighty God according to the dictates of their own consciences and understanding: And that no man ought or of right can be compelled to attend any religious worship, or erect or support any place of worship, or maintain any ministry, contrary to, or against, his own free will and consent: Nor can any man, who acknowledges the being of a God, be justly deprived or abridged of any civil right as a citizen, on account of his religious sentiments or peculiar mode of religious worship: And that no authority can or ought to be vested in, or assumed by any power whatever, that shall in any case interfere with, or in any manner controul, the right of conscience in the free exercise of religious worship.

III. That the people of this State have the sole, exclusive and inherent right of governing and regulating the internal police of the same.

IV. That all power being originally inherent in, and consequently derived from, the people; therefore all officers of government, whether legislative or executive, are their trustees and servants, and at all times accountable to them.

V. That government is, or ought to be, instituted for the common benefit, protection and security of the people, nation or community; and not for the particular emolument or advantage of any single man, family, or soft of men, who are a part only of that community, And that the community hath an indubitable, unalienable and indefeasible right to reform, alter, or abolish government in such manner as shall be by that community judged most conducive to the public weal.

VI. That those who are employed in the legislative and executive business of the State, may be restrained from oppression, the people have a right, at such periods as they may think proper, to reduce their public officers to a private station, and supply the vacancies by certain and regular elections.

VII. That all elections ought to be free; and that all free men having a sufficient evident common interest with, and attachment to the community, have a right to elect officers, or to be elected into office.

VIII. That every member of society hath a right to be protected in the enjoyment of life, liberty and property, and therefore is bound to contribute his proportion towards the expence of that protection, and yield his personal service when necessary, or an equivalent thereto: But no part of a man's property can be justly taken from him, or applied to public uses, without his own consent, or that of his legal representatives: Nor can any man who is conscientiously scrupulous of bearing arms, be justly compelled thereto, if he will pay such equivalent, nor are the people bound by any laws, but such as they have in like manner assented to, for their common good.

IX. That in all prosecutions for criminal offences, a man hath a right to be heard by himself and his council, to demand the cause and nature of his accusation, to be confronted with the witnesses, to call for evidence in his favour, and a speedy public trial, by an impartial jury of the country, without the unanimous consent of which jury he cannot be found guilty; nor can he be compelled to give evidence against himself; nor can any man be justly deprived of his liberty except by the laws of the land, or the judgment of his peers.

X. That the people have a right to hold themselves, their houses, papers, and possessions free from search and seizure, and therefore warrants without oaths or affirmations first made, affording a sufficient foundation for them, and whereby any officer or messenger may be commanded or required to search suspected places, or to seize any person or persons, his or their property, not particularly described, are contrary to that right, and ought not to be granted.

XI. That in controversies respecting property, and in suits between man and man, the parties have a right to trial by jury, which ought to be held sacred.

XII. That the people have a right to freedom of speech, and of writing, and publishing their sentiments; therefore the freedom of the press ought not to be restrained.

XIII. That the people have a right to bear arms for the defence of themselves and the state; and as standing armies in the time of peace are dangerous to liberty, they ought not to be kept up; And that the military should be kept under strict subordination to, and governed by, the civil power.

XIV. That a frequent recurrence to fundamental principles, and a firm adherence to justice, moderation, temperance, industry, and frugality are absolutely necessary to preserve the blessings of liberty, and keep a government free: The people ought therefore to pay particular attention to these points in the choice of officers and representatives, and have a right to exact a due and constant regard to them, from their legislatures and magistrates, in the making and executing such laws as are necessary for the good government of the state.

XV. That all men have a natural inherent right to emigrate from one state to another that will receive them, or to form a new state in vacant countries, or in such countries as they can purchase, whenever they think that thereby they may promote their own happiness.

XVI. That the people have a right to assemble together, to consult for their common good, to instruct their representatives, and to apply to the legislature for redress of grievances, by address, petition, or remonstrance.

Constitution of North Carolina : December 18, 1776

A DECLARATION OF RIGHTS, &C.

I. That all political power is vested in and derived from the people only.

II. That the people of this State ought to have the sole and exclusive right of regulating the internal government and police thereof.

III. That no man or set of men are entitled to exclusive or separate emoluments or privileges from the community, but in consideration of public services.

IV. That the legislative, executive, and supreme judicial powers of government, ought to be forever separate and distinct from each other.

V. That all powers of suspending laws, or the execution of laws, by any authority, without consent of the Representatives of the people, is injurious to their rights, and ought not to be exercised.

VI. That elections of members, to serve as Representatives in General Assembly, ought to be free.

VII. That, in all criminal prosecutions, every man has a right to be informed of the accusation against him, and to confront the accusers and witnesses with other testimony, and shall not be compelled to give evidence against himself.

VIII. That no freeman shall be put to answer any criminal charge, but by indictment, presentment, or impeachment.

IX. That no freeman shall be convicted of any crime, but by the unanimous verdict of a jury of good and lawful men, in open court, as heretofore used.

X. That excessive bail should not be required, nor excessive fines imposed, nor cruel or unusual punishments inflicted.

XI. That general warrants -- whereby an officer or messenger may he commanded to search suspected places, without evidence of the fact conmlittecl, or to seize any person or persons, not named, whose offences are not particularly described, and supported by evidence -- are dangerous to liberty, and ought not to be granted.

XII. That no freeman ought to be taken, imprisoned, or disseized of his freehold liberties or privileges, or outlawed, or exiled, or in any nlanller destroyed, or deprived of his life, liberty, or property, but by the law of the land.

XIII. That every freeman, restrained of his liberty, is entitled to a remedy, to inquire into the lawfulness thereof, and to remove the same, if unlawful; and that such remedy ought not to be denied or delayed.

XIV. That in all controversies at law, respecting property, the ancient mode of trial, by jury, is one of the best securities of the rights of the people, and ought to remain sacred and inviolable.

XV. That the freedom of the press is one of the great bulwarks of liberty, and therefore ought never to he restrained.

XVI. That the people of this State ought not to be taxed, or made subject to the payment of any impost or duty, without the consent of themselves, or their Representatives in General Assembly, freely given.

XVII. That the people have a right to bear arms, for the defence of the State; and, as standing armies, in time of peace, are danger-ous to liberty, they ought not to be kept up; and that the military should be kept under strict subordination to, and governed by, the civil power.

XVIII. That the people have a right to assemble together, to consult for their common good, to instruct their Representatives, and to apply to the Legislature, for redress of grievances.

XIX. That all men have a natural and unalienable right to worship Almighty God according to the dictates of their own consciences.

XX. That, for redress of grievances, and for amending and strengthening the laws, elections ought to be often held.

XXI. That a frequent recurrence to fundamental principles is absolutely necessary, to preserve the blessings of liberty.

XXII. That no hereditary emoluments, privileges or honors ought to be granted or conferred in this State.

XXIII. That perpetuities and monopolies are contrary to the genius of a free State, and ought not to be allowed.

XXIV. That retrospective laws, punishing facts committed before the existence of such laws, and by them only declared criminal, are oppressive, unjust, and incompatible with liberty; wherefore no ex post facto law ought to be made.

XXV. The property of the soil, in a free government, being one of the essential rights of the collective body of the people, it is necessary, in order to avoid future disputes, that the limits of the State should be ascertained with precision; and as the former temporary line between North and South Carolina, was confirmed, and extended by Commissioners, appointed by the Legislatures of the two States, agreeable to the order of the late King George the Second, in Council, that line, and that only, should be esteemed the southern boundary of this State as follows: that is to say, beginning on the sea side, at a cedar stake, at or near the mouth of Little River (being the southern extremity of Brunswick county) and running from thence a northwest course, through the boundary house, which stands in thirty-three degrees fifty-six minutes, to thirty-five degrees north latitude; and from thence a west course so far as is mentioned in the Charter of King Charles the Second, to the late Proprietors of Carolina. Therefore all the territories, seas, waters, and harbours, with their appurtenances, lying between the line above described, and the southern line of the State of Virginia, which begins on the sea shore, in thirty-six degrees thirty minutes, north latitude, and from thence runs west, agreeable to the said Charter of King Charles, are the right and property of the people of this State, to be held by them in sovereignty; any partial line, without the consent of the Legislature of this State, at any time thereafter directed, or laid out, in anywise notwithstanding: -- Provided always, That this Declaration of Rights shall not prejudice any nation or nations of Indians, from enjoying such hunting-grounds as may have been, or hereafter shall be, secured to them by any former or future Legislature of this State: -- And provided also, That it shall not be construed so as to prevent the establishment of one or more governments westward of this State, by consent of the Legislature: -- And provided further, That nothing herein contained shall affect the titles or repossessions of individuals holding or claiming under the laws heretofore in force, or grants heretofore made by the late King George the Second, or his predecessors, or the late lords proprietors, or any of them.

Constitution of Maryland : November 11, 1776

A Declaration of Rights, and the Constitution and Form of Government agreed to by the Delegates of Maryland, in Free and Full Convention Assembled.

A DECLARATION OF RIGHTS, &C.

THE parliament of Great Britain, by a declaratory act, having assumed a right to make laws to bind the Colonies in all cases whatsoever, and, in pursuance of Rich claim, endeavoured, by force of arms, to subjugate the United Colonies to an unconditional submission to their will and power, and having at length constrained them to declare themselves independent States, and to assume government under the authority of the people; Therefore we, the Delegates of Maryland, in free and full Convention assembled, taking into our most serious consideration the best means of establishing a good Constitution in this State, for the sure foundation and more permanent security thereof, declare,

I. That all government of right originates from the people, is founded in compact only, and instituted solely for the good of the whole.

II. That the people of this State ought to have the sole and exclusive right of regulating the internal government and police thereof.

III. That the inhabitants of Maryland are entitled to the common law of England, and the trial by Jury, according that law, and to the benefit of such of the English statutes, as existed at the time of their first emigration, and which, by experience, have been found applicable to their local and other circumstances, and of such others as have been since made in England, or Great Britain, and have been introduced, used and practiced by the courts of law or equity; and also to acts of Assembly, in force on the first of June seventeen hundred and seventy-four, except such as may have since expired, or have been or may be altered by facts of Convention, or this Declaration of Rights-subject, nevertheless, to the revision of, and Amendment or repeal by, the Legislature of this State: and the inhabitants of Maryland are also entitled to all property, derived to them, from or under the Charter, granted by his Majesty Charles I. to Crecilius Calvert, Baron of Baltimore.

IV. That all persons invested with the legislative or executive powers of government are the trustees of the public, and, as such, accountable for their conduct; wherefore, whenever the ends of government are perverted, and public liberty manifestly endangered, and all other means of redress are ineffectual, the people may, and of right ought, to reform the old or establish a new government. The doctrine of non-resistance, against arbitrary power and oppression, is absurd, slavish, and destructive of the good and happiness of mankind.

V. That the right in the people to participate in the Legislature is the best security of liberty, and the foundation of all free government; for this purpose, elections ought to be free and frequent, and every man, having property in, a common interest with, and an attachment to the community, ought to have a right of suffrage.

VI. That the legislative, executive and judicial powers of government, ought to be forever separate and distinct from each other.

VII. That no power of suspending laws, or the execution of laws, unless by or derived from the Legislature, ought to be exercised or allowed.

VIII. That freedom of speech and debates, or proceedings in the Legislature, ought not to be impeached in any other court or judicature.

IX. That a place for the meeting of the Legislature ought to be fixed, the most convenient to the members thereof, and to the depository of public records; and the Legislature ought not to be convened or held at any other place, but from evident necessity.

X. That, for redress of grievances, and for amending, strengthening and preserving the laws, the Legislature ought to be frequently convened.

XI. That every man hath a right to petition the Legislature, for the redress of grievances, in a peaceable and orderly manner.

XII. That no aid, charge, tax, fee, or fees, ought to be set, rated, or levied, under any presence, without consent of the Legislature.

XIII. That the levying taxes by the poll is grievous and oppressive, and ought to be abolished; that paupers ought not to be assessed for the support of government; but every other person in the State ought to contribute his proportion of public taxes, for the support of government, according to his actual worth, in real or personal property, within the State; yet fines, duties, or taxes, may properly and justly be imposed or laid, with a political view, for the good government and benefit of the community.

XIV. That sanguinary laws ought to be avoided, as far as is Consistent with the safety of the State: and no law, to inflict cruel and unusual pains and penalties, ought to be made in any case, or at any time hereafter.

XV. That retrospective laws, punishing facts committed before the existence of such laws, and by them only declared criminal, are oppressive, unjust, and incompatible with liberty; wherefore no *ex post facto* law ought to be made.

XVI. That no law, to attains particular persons of treason or felony, ought to be made in any case, or at any time hereafter.

XVII. That every freeman, for any injury done him in his person or property, ought to have remedy, by the course of the law of the land, and ought to have justice and right freely without sale, fully without any denial, and speedily without delay, according to the law of the land.

XVIII. That the trial of facts where they arise, is one of the greatest securities of the lives, liberties and estates of the people.

XIX. That, in all criminal prosecutions, every man hath a right to be informed of the accusation against him; to have a copy of the indictment or charge in due time (if required) to prepare for his defence; to be allowed counsel; to be confronted with the witnesses against him; to have process for his witnesses; to examine the witnesses, for and against him, on oath; and to a speedy trial by an impartial jury, without whose unanimous consent he ought not to be found guilty.

XX. That no man ought to be compelled to give evidence against himself, in a common court of law, or in any other court, but in such cases as have been usually practiced in this State, or may hereafter be directed by the Legislature.

XXI. That no freeman ought to be taken, or imprisoned, or disseized of his freehold, liberties, or privileges, or outlawed, or exiled, or in any manner destroyed, or deprived of his life, liberty, or property, but by the judgment of his peers, or by the law of the land.

XXII. That excessive bail ought not to be required, nor excessive fines imposed, nor cruel or unusual punishments inflicted, by the courts of law.

XXIII. That all warrants, without oath or affirmation, to search suspected places, or to seize any person or property, are grievous and oppressive; and all general warrants-to search suspected places, or to apprehend suspected persons, without naming or describing the place, or the person in special-are illegal, and ought not to be granted.

XXIV. That there ought to be no forfeiture of any part of the estate of any person, for any crime except murder, or treason against the State, and then only on conviction and attainder.

XXV. That a well-regulated militia is the proper and natural defence of a free government.

XXVI. That standing armies are dangerous to liberty, and ought not to be raised or kept up, without consent of the Legislature.

XXVII. That in all cases, and at all times, the military ought to be under strict subordination to and control of the civil power.

XXVIII. That no soldier ought to be quartered in any house, in time of peace, without the consent of the owner; and in time of war, in such manner only, as the Legislature shall direct,

XXIX. That no person, except regular soldiers, mariners, and marines in the service of this State, or militia when in actual service, ought in any case to be subject to or punishable by martial law.

XXX. That the independency and uprightness of Judges are essential to the impartial administration of Justice, and a great security to the rights and liberties of the people; wherefore the Chancellor and Judges ought to hold commissions during good behaviour; and the said Chancellor and Judges shall be removed for misbehaviour, on conviction in a court of law, and may be removed by the Governor, upon the address of the General Assembly; *Provided,*That two-thirds of all the members of each House concur in such address. That salaries, liberal, but not profuse, ought to be secured to the Chancellor and the Judges, during the continuance of their Commissions, in such manner, and at such times, as the Legislature shall hereafter direct, upon consideration of the circumstances of this State. No Chancellor or Judge ought to hold any other office, civil or military, or receive fees or perquisites of any kind.

XXXI. That a long continuance in the first executive departments of power or trust, is dangerous to liberty; a rotation, therefore, in those departments, is one of the best securities of permanent freedom.

XXXII. That no person ought to hold, at the same time, more shall one office of profit, nor ought any person. in public trust, to receive any present from any foreign prince or state, or from the United States, or any of them, without the approbation of this State.

XXXIII. That, as it is the duty of every man to worship God in such manner as he thinks most acceptable to him; all persons, professing the Christian religion, are equally entitled to protection in their religious liberty; wherefore no person ought by any law to be molested in his person or estate on account of his religious persuasion or profession, or for his religious practice; unless, under colour of religion, any man shall disturb the good order, peace or safety of the State, or shall infringe the laws of morality, or injure others, in their natural, civil, or religious rights; nor ought any person to be compelled to frequent or maintain, or contribute, unless on contract, to maintain any particular place of worship, or any particular ministry; yet the Legislature may, in their discretion, lay a general and equal tax for the support of the Christian religion; leaving to each individual the power of appointing the payment over of the money, collected from him, to the support of any particular place of worship or minister, or for the benefit of the poor of his own denomination, or the poor in general of any particular county: but the churches, chapels, globes, and all other property now belonging to the church of England, ought to remain to the church of England forever. And all acts of Assembly, lately passed, for collecting monies for building or repairing particular churches or chapels of ease, shall continue in force, and be executed, unless the Legislature shall, by act, supersede or repeal the same: but no county court shall assess any quantity of tobacco, or sum of money, hereafter, on the application of any vestrymen or church-wardens; and every encumbent of the church of England, who hath remained in his parish, and performed his duty, shall be entitled to receive the provision and support established by the act, entitled "An act for the support of the clergy of the church of England, in this Province," till the November court of this present year to be held for the county in which his parish shall lie, or partly lie, or for such time as he hate remained in his parish, and performed his duty.

XXXIV. That every gift, sale, or devise of lands, to any minister, public teacher, or preacher of the gospel, as such, or to any religious sect, order or denomination, or to or for the support, use or benefit of, or in trust for, any minister, public teacher, or preacher of the gospel, as such, or any religious sect, order or denomination-and every gift or sale of good-e, or chattels, to go in succession, or to take place after the death of the seller or donor, or to or for such support, use or benefit-and also every devise of goods or chattels to or for the support, use or benefit of any minister, public teacher, or preacher of the gospel, as such, or any religious sect, order, or denomination, without the leave of the Legislature, shall be void; except always any sale, gift, lease or devise of any quantity of land, not exceeding two acres, for a church, meeting, or other house of worship, and for a burying-ground, which shall be improved, enjoyed or used only for such purpose-or such sale, gift, lease, or devise, shall be void.

XXXV. That no other test or qualification ought to be required, on admission to any office of trust or profit, than such oath of support and fidelity to this State, and such oath of office, as shall be directed by this Convention or the Legislature of this State, and a declaration of a belief in the Christian religion.

XXXVI. That the manner of administering an oath to any person, ought to be such, as those of the religious persuasion, profession, or denomination, of which such person is one, generally esteem the most effectual confirmation, by the attestation of the Divine Being. And that the people called Quakers, those called Dunkers, and those called Menonists, holding it unlawful to take an oath on any occasion, ought to be allowed to make their solemn affirmation, in the manner that Quakers 1lave been heretofore allowed to affirm; and to be of the same avail as an oath, in all such cases, as the affirmation of Quakers hath been allowed and accepted within this State, instead of an oath. And further, on such affirmation, warrants to search for stolen goods, or for the apprehension or commitment of offenders, ought to be granted, or security for the peace awarded, and Quakers, Dunkers or Menonists ought also, on their solemn affirmation as aforesaid, to be admitted as witnesses, in all criminal cases not capital.

XXXVII. That the city of Annapolis ought to have all its rights, privileges and benefits, agreeable to its Charter, and the acts of Assembly confirming and regulating the same, subject nevertheless to such alteration as may be made by this Convention, or any future legislature.

XXXVIII. That the liberty of the press ought to be inviolably preserved.

XXXIX. That monopolies are odious, contrary to the spirit of a free government, and the principles of commerce; and ought not to be suffered.

XL. That no title of nobility, or hereditary honours, ought to be granted III this State.

XLI. That the subsisting resolves of this and the several Conventions held for this Colony, ought to be in force as laws, unless altered by this Convention, or the Legislature of this State.

XLII. That this Declaration of Rights, or the Form of Government, to be established by this Convention, or any part or either of them, ought not to be altered, changed or abolished, by the Legislature of this State, but in such manner as this Convention shall prescribe and direct.

NOTES

[1] The extent to which national political parties use propaganda to influence voters is rampant. My 1983 American Heritage Dictionary defines propaganda as "ideas, information or other material disseminated to win people over to a given doctrine." In national politics, the end of the sentence should be changed to read "... to win people over to vote for a given candidate or party." Some examples are particularly odious.

- President George W. Bush thought he might attract voters by describing himself as a compassionate conservative. Much like hope and change, compassionate conservative is a meaningless and ambiguous term: compassionate about what and conservative on what? Compassionate conservative is a joke to modern liberals and anathema to conservatives. People are compassionate or not, irrespective of their political philosophy. To ascribe governing as compassionate is cover for taking other people's money and giving it to others. Such redistribution may be appropriate for governments, but to rationalize it with the label of compassion is disingenuous.

- Modern Liberals hijacked the progressive label some time ago to deflect their brand away from modern liberalism to one that seems inarguable: progress. But in reality, as T.S. Eliot observed (in the 1930s, no less), modern liberals are embarked on "... an age which advances progressively backwards." Real American progress is enhancing the general welfare not promoting centralized governmental planning and control over individual freedom and liberty.

[2] If the reader has not yet noted, this author believes that the vast majority of Americans, including the vast majority of politicians, and those who support individual politicians or political parties, are people of integrity and motivated to do the best for the country and its people. From this perspective, it follows that the evolution of the American political system has been the result of political leaders and

government officials doing their best, and doing what they thought would provide positive results. (The exception to this rosy attitude was, of course, the racist motivations of both State and Federal officials following the Civil War until the 1960s or later. It is impossible to say when this exception came to an end. From my view, however, it is at an end today.)

I believe this attitude is both healthy and liberating. It is healthy because it encourages individuals to treat one another with dignity and respect no matter their political leanings or affiliations. It is liberating because it allows an individual to look past the motivations of those with different opinions about the size, structure and activities of government, and to honestly understand their concerns, and their view of the problems facing their community, their State and their country.

So, it must follow that if politicians and both parties had the greatest of intentions and were trying to do their best, the reasons that the Federal government is in crisis must be due to a governance construct that wasn't, and isn't, encouraging effective governance, nor is it properly supporting and incentivizing politicians to enact laws and appropriate funds to meet the true needs and expectations of the electorate.

Those who adopt today's pundit-condensed, blog-inspired reasoning or prescriptions, right or left, will probably never believe that what has gotten us to where we are hasn't been conspiracies, or money, or the elites, but rather governmental structural defects that have not weathered well. The old saying is that representative democratic government is flawed and imperfect, but remains the best system of government. Key word here is *system*. Our system has grown obsolete.

[3] The Federal income tax started in 1913. It was very simple and was focused on the wealthy and the very wealthy. There were no separate capital gains taxes and no deductions. There were two exemptions: one for married couples filing jointly, and one for individuals. The original exemptions were $4,000 and $3,000. Adjusting 1913 dollars to today's dollars, the exemptions would be about $89,000 (couple) and $67,000 (single). If an individual's income was more than $67,000, the tax was 1% on the amount of income up to about

$456,000. The tax rate was 2% for income above $456,000, 3% for income above $1.1M, 4% for income above $1.7M, 5% for income above $2.3M, 6% for income above $5.75M, and 7% for income above $11.5M. In today's parlance, it was a tax on the 1% and didn't affect the 99%.

[4] United States v. Wrightwood Dairy Company, 315 U.S. 110 (1942), Opinion by Chief Justice Harlan F. Stone.

[5] United States v. Alfonso Lopez, Jr., 514 U.S. 549 (1995). Opinion by Chief Justice William Rehnquist.

[6] Your Senator or Congressman will jump on this statement. They will cite the Leahy-Smith American Invents Act, which was passed by both Houses and signed into law in September 2011. But this is the first change in patent law in 60 years. A functioning government would review and assess one of its main governing functions on a regular basis, not every half century. Additionally, it will be months before it is seen if the new law achieves what it intended to achieve, and to see what its unintended consequences will be. The government will be worthy of a pat on the back if Congress or the President assess the new law in a year or two and make changes. I suspect they won't do so until, maybe, 2050, unless the governmental system is changed.

[7] Article I, Section 8 lists the powers of Congress, which together are commonly known as the enumerated powers. Section 9 of Article I lists actions that the Federal government cannot take, such as passing an ex post facto law, and Section 10 lists actions that States are prohibited from taking, such as entering into a treaty.

[8] A "non-profit" organization is structurally no different than any business enterprise, whether a private company or a public corporation. For any enterprise to stay in business, revenues must meet or exceed expenses. Those who manage an organization effectively ensure that revenues exceed expenditures each year, both to make sure that it can cover annual expenses, and to build a reserve that might be needed in the future. The excess of revenues over expenditures is profit. The profit earned by a private company or public corporation is subject to taxes. The profit earned by a non-profit is not. In other words, the only significant difference between "for-profit" and "non-profit" enterprises is not comparable in terms of profit; it is

that the former pays taxes while the "non-profit" pays no taxes. It would be more correct to label a "non-profit" a "non-taxed."

The profits earned by taxed versus non-taxed enterprises are used differently. Taxed enterprises are motivated to avoid taxable profit, whereas a non-taxed enterprise has no such motivation. Assuming that government tax rules exist not just to generate government revenue, but also to effect government policy, it is evident that government can influence the behavior of a taxed enterprise (effect government policy), whereas a non-taxed enterprise is not influenced by the government's policies embedded in a tax code.

For both taxed and non-taxed enterprises, employee wages and salaries are an expense. To maintain a positive ratio of revenues to expenditures, both types of enterprises have an incentive to provide competitive wages and salaries for employees, not overly-generous ones. Incentives tend to limit the salary of the CEO of a taxed enterprise because the owners of the company collect more money, the company's profit, if the CEO salary (an expense) is lower. If the CEO is the sole owner, the CEO would rather earn company profits than earn a large salary, the latter usually being taxed at a higher rate. Even if the CEO is a part owner, incentives tend toward improving profit rather than the CEO's salary level. The CEO of a non-taxed enterprise has an incentive for a large personal salary. The non-taxed enterprise CEO has no share in profits, even though the CEO's performance is tied to the effectiveness of the CEO in raising revenue. The non-taxed CEO can only be rewarded with salary.

Finally, most non-taxed enterprises, like many taxed enterprises, are service organizations. Non-taxed enterprises pay employees to provide services or to pursue activities, and some non-taxed enterprises expend some of their revenues in buying things for others or disbursing grants. A taxed service-providing enterprise isn't in the business of giving away cash. When expenditures (salaries or wages) of a taxed enterprise exceed revenues, employees are fired or their hours are reduced. When non-taxed enterprises have revenue shortfalls, they usually reduce their cash distributions and retain their employees. Most of the employees, after all, are the solicitors for donations to the enterprise. For the non-taxed enterprise, cutting employees reduces revenue capacity.

Of course, most non-profits are well-run enterprises that seek to deliver goods and services with low overhead, just like most businesses seek to minimize overhead in order to improve profitability. The board of directors of a non-profit limits the profitability of the non-profit; the market place limits the profitability of a taxed company. But of course there are greedy, unscrupulous companies that seek to maximize profits at any cost. And there are greedy, unscrupulous non-profits that seek to maximize employee salaries, benefits and expense accounts.

[9] Treasurydirect.gov

[10] The calculations supporting this number are found on page 39.

[11] The data was compiled by the web site USgovernmentspending. com. The 2010 numbers include some that are estimated, since not all the databases compiled by the government for Fiscal Year 2010, which ended on 30 September 2010, are yet complete. (I wrote this note in December 2011; over a year after the end of the fiscal year, the federal accountants still hadn't finished and published their books – interesting.) In doing the research for this book, I looked into numerous sources for a reliable and accurate record of local, state and federal revenues and expenditures (usually labeled outlays in federal budgeting). The data is there; but it is far from being 'user-friendly.' The web site, a private one, on the other hand, makes processing data commensurate with the advanced state of computerized databases. It is probably telling that the federal government can't produce a web site that is as transparent. My experience with the State of Virginia, where strict accounting is actually important, I hope is typical of other State government accounting agencies. For residents of Virginia, if you want to know where each State tax dollar is going, and also where each local tax dollar is going, in spreadsheets that permit comparison, visit the Virginia Auditor of Public Accounts' web site, www.apa.state.va.us. The accounting is timely, thorough, and easy to understand.

[12] Teddy Roosevelt gave his famous speech on August 31, 1910 at Osawatomie, Kansas during a two-day ceremony to dedicate a park commemorating the abolitionist John Brown. President Obama cited the speech and quoted from it in a speech he gave at Osawatomie in December 2011. Historian Robert S. La Forte described the essence

of TR's speech by quoting this extract from it:

> The American people are right in demanding a new National-
> ism without which we cannot hope to deal with new problems.
> The new Nationalism puts the National need before sectional
> or personal advantage. It is impatient of the utter confusion
> that results from local legislatures attempting to treat National
> issues as local issues. It is still more impatient of the impotence
> which springs from over-division of governmental powers, the
> impotence which makes it possible for local selfishness or for
> legal cunning, hired by wealthy special interests, to bring Na-
> tional activities to a deadlock. This new Nationalism regards
> the executive power as the steward of public welfare. It de-
> mands of the judiciary that it shall be interested primarily in
> human welfare rather than in property, just as it demands that
> the representative body shall represent all the people rather
> than any one class or section of the people.

There is general agreement that TR was calling for a more active and
powerful Federal government. But it is inaccurate to cite the speech
as calling for federal preeminence. In his Osawatomie speech, President Obama quoted from TR's speech twice. The first quote was:
"Our country means nothing unless it means the triumph of a real
democracy ... of an economic system under which each man shall
be guaranteed the opportunity to show the best that there is in him."
The full quote is (with the missing words in italics): "Our country,
this great republic, means nothing unless it means the triumph of a
real democracy, *the triumph of popular government, and, in the long
run*, of an economic system under which each man shall be guaranteed the opportunity to show the best that there is in him."

Toward the end of his speech, President Obama took the following
quote from TR's speech: "We are all Americans. Our common interests are as broad as the continent." This quote includes the second
and third sentences of a paragraph that began with, "I do not ask
for overcentralization; but I do ask that we work in a spirit of broad
and far-reaching nationalism when we work for what concerns our
people as a whole."

[13] The applicability of some portions of the Constitution to State

governments is an area which is a matter of legal debate. The issue generally involves the provisions of Section 9, Article I, and the Bill of Rights. I think one of the more interesting specific instances which highlight that States were not intended to be bound by Section 9 concerns the prohibition against granting a Title of Nobility. Section 9 states, "No Title of Nobility shall be granted by the United States." Section 10 states, "No State shall ... grant any Title of Nobility." The writers and ratifiers of the Constitution explicitly prescribed the power of both the Federal government and State governments: in this case, to assign a title of nobility. Why would they explicitly define a Federal and State power? Simple; because all the other descriptions of powers were predicated on the basis that powers not assigned to the Federal government were never intended for the Federal government.

[14] After reconstruction, state-sponsored racism took root despite the new Constitutional prohibitions against it. This further illustrates the need for Constitutional language to be explicit and precise in setting rules and guidelines.

[15] The idea that a Constitutional Convention should be avoided because it might do more harm than good is not new. Gales and Seaton's history of the debates in Congress includes discussion on this very topic when the first Congress was debating the proposed new Bill of Rights. The history paraphrases what Congressman Thomas A. Tucker said on August 18, 1789. "Five important States have pretty plainly expressed their apprehensions of the danger to which the rights of their citizens are exposed. Finding these cannot be secured in the mode they had wished, they will naturally recur to the alternative, and endeavor to obtain a federal convention; the consequence of this may be disagreeable to the Union; party spirit may be revived, and animosities rekindled destructive of tranquility. States that exert themselves to obtain a federal convention, and those that oppose the measure, may feel so strongly the spirit of discord, as to sever the Union asunder. If in this conflict the advocates for a federal convention should prove successful, the consequences may be alarming; we may lose many of the valuable principles now established in the present constitution. (Page 787, A Century of Lawmaking for a New Nation: U.S. Congressional Documents and Debates, 1774-1875.)

Contrast Tucker's views with what Hamilton wrote in Federalist Paper 85. "But every Amendment to the Constitution ... would be a single proposition, and might be brought forward singly. There would be no necessity for management or compromise in relation to any other point. ... There can, therefore, be no comparison between the facility of affecting an Amendment and that of establishing, in the first instance, a complete Constitution."

[16] Wickard v. Filburn, 317 U.S. 111 (1942). At the time, the Federal government had set quotas for how much wheat could be grown in trying to keep wheat prices at certain levels. Filburn's quota was to plant ten acres. He actually planted more, and claimed the excess was for his personal use. The Supreme Court declared that home-grown wheat competes with wheat in commerce, so the Federal government did have the power to regulate home-grown produce.

[17] I heartily recommend Dan Farber's book on the Ninth Amendment. Even after exhaustively examining its history, I believe that he is still scratching his head about the 200 hundred year irrelevance of this Amendment. I like to call it the appendix Amendment; it's there, but is apparently useless. Dan Farber, "Retained by the People: The "Silent" Ninth Amendment and the Constitutional Rights Americans Don't Know They Have," 2007.

[18] Federalist Paper 62, probably James Madison; The Federalist Papers, New American Library, NAL Penguin, NY, NY, 1961.

[19] Ratification of the Constitution by the State of Rhode Island, May 29, 1790, http:Avalon.lay.yale.edu/18th_century.

[20] Ratification of the Constitution by the State of New York, July 26, 1788, http:Avalon.lay.yale.edu/18th_century.

[21] This is speculation on my part. But I am willing to bet that my guess is probably right. It was no less than Mr. Norris himself, within days of the legislation taking effect, addressed the new legislative body and suggested that the representatives be given the title of Senator. It became law.

[22] State of Nebraska state web site, http://nebraskalegislature.gov/about/history_unicameral.php.

[23] German Government web site; http://www.tatsachen-ueber-deutschland.de/en/political-system/main-content-04

[24] It would help if there was an incentive to dangle in front of elect-

ed representatives who would lose their seats in the transition to a unicameral legislature. One option would be to do what many local governments do: have most representatives selected by district voters, but have a number of seats based on at-large representation. Here's another idea that might provide a venue for their employment that would serve a truly useful purpose and would allow them to retain a position (and a title) reflective of government officialdom. I would advise the creation of Regional Advisory Councils, or RACs, comprised of a small number of representatives of from each of the states in each RAC. Because the Constitution prohibits us from titling them Lord, or Duke, we'd have to settle on calling them Senator. Aside from the human aspect, however, regional councils could in fact serve a useful function by making recommendations on State legislation that has regional implications, and to make recommendations to State legislators on issues and initiatives with regional concerns that are obvious at the State level. The councils would also serve as a clearinghouse to identify successful State laws that other States should consider adopting.

I would propose 9 RACs, whose states share similar economic, geographic and topographical characteristics:
New England: ME, NH, MA, RI, CT.
Great Lakes East: NY, PA, OH.
Great Lakes West: MI, IN, IL, WI.
Atlantic: NJ, DE, MD, VA, NC, SC.
Gulf: FL, GA, AL, MS, LA
Missouri River: ND, SD, NE, MN, AI, MO, AR.
South Central: TX, OK.
Great West: MT, ID, WY, UT, CO, KS, AZ, NM, NV.
Pacific: WA, OR, CA, AK, HI,